TIME, BEING, AND SOUL IN THE OLDEST SANSKRIT SOURCES

William Snyder

Center for Medieval and Renaissance Studies
Institute of Global Cultural Studies
Asian and Asian American Studies
Global Publications
2001

Library of Congress Cataloging-in-Publication Data

William Snyder
Time, Being, and Soul in the Oldest Sanskrit Sources

1. Being 2. Time
3. Hinduism 4. Indo-European Languages

ISBN 1-586840-72-X

Published and distributed by
Center for Medieval and Renaissance Studies
Institute of Global Cultural Studies
Asian and Asian American Studies
Global Publications, Binghamton University
Binghamton, New York, USA 13902-6000
Phone: (607) 777-4495. Fax: 777-6132
E-mail: pmorewed@binghamton.edu
http://ssips.binghamton.edu

Table of Contents

ACKNOWLEDGEMENTS

This volume reflects my years of interest in Sanskrit Literature, Hindu culture and particularly wonders at the greatness of the authors of the ancient texts – particularly of the Rig Veda. But the publication of my thoughts and speculations on the topics I have taken up here are the result of the insistent prompting from my friend and colleague Parvis Morewedge and I owe him endless thanks for his unrelenting efforts.

I also wish to thank Norma Heslep whose help in editing my writing with her rare skills in the English language have surely saved me much embarrassment.

W.H.S.

SOME NOTES ON THE TRANSLITERATION OF SANSKRIT TEXTS:

1. In Sanskrit the word final –*vowel* + *m* changes to a nasalized vowel before the initial consonant of the following word, e.g., *tam bhūtam.* In Sanskrit this is written as anusvāra (i.e., as · over the preceding consonant). But westerners have traditionally transcribed this nasalized vowel as: *m* with the · above it, but I have chosen to transcribe it with the symbol for the nasalized vowel instead, e.g., with ã, because the traditional transcript seems to suggest that the nasal *m* is still present.
2. The Sanskrit alphabet - and the ancient Sanskrit scholars as well - recognized two distinctly different –*r* sounds, one a consonant and one a vowel. The vowel sound occurs only between consonants while the consonant is found joined to a vowel. The vowel has traditionally been transcribed as ṛ, but I find that many of our Indian colleagues now use the consonant symbol for this sound since it is essentially unambiguous. I have followed their example, e.g., in *grha*- 'house'; the -*r*- must be a vowel, but in *rabh*- 'take' it can only be a consonant.
3. Word final -*s* becomes an unvoiced vowel in sentence final position. This has conventionally been transcribed as -*ḥ*, but simply using the normal -*h*- here saves the type setter a great deal of difficulty - especially in the US where - in my experience - typesetters have little interest in producing these complicated characters.
4. The character ṇ represents the Sanskrit retroflex nasal; *ṣ* represents the Sanskrit retroflex sibilant; *ṭ* represents the unvoiced retroflex stop, *ḍ* represents the voiced retroflex stop.

INTRODUCTION

The purpose of this study is to isolate and define the early advances of Hindu culture in speculations on the nature of *being*, *time*, and *soul*. What Hindu thinkers in their speculations were able to achieve may seem but slight in the light of later historical development and of our inclination to see others only in the context of our own cultural preferences. But the initial stages of the original thought of the early Hindus provide insight into the origins of the world and the problems that arise in seeking a resolution of the questions surrounding these most fundamental of all subjects. True, not only later Hindu seers, but other thinkers throughout the world have also attempted to resolve these very same mysteries without achieving any significant advances beyond what the original Hindu thinkers achieved.

I have approached this question primarily from a philological perspective for it is from the historical, written and spoken evidence at our disposal that we are able to understand how the Hindu seers went about defining and resolving questions about the nature of the world, i.e., of being, time, and soul. These questions have occupied men's minds from the earliest days of recorded time and on to the present day. From the linguistic evidence we are able to discern what the Hindu thinkers precisely achieved and how they expressed their new perceptions of the world and its origin. From the meanings of the texts through which we gain insight into their speculations, we can fully understand the meaning of the ideas that they present by making use of the philological tools that we have at our disposal. In virtually every culture that we know of, the unpredictable forces of nature, those elements which plague man's existence or which provide man with the basic necessities of life, have been anthropomorphized, deified, and transformed into objects of religious veneration. Man has always sought to dominate violent, hostile and sometimes, even benevolent forces through religious rituals, i.e., through the appeals to these anthropomorphized forces, efforts to control them through magic. But the search for answers to the far more profound questions, such as the the mystifying and perplexing fact of death and the equally puzzling question of the origin of every thing that exists is also commonly relegated to the area of religious dogma. These answers are to be sought in that force or amongst those forces, which control all other forces of nature. Modern thought has removed nature's forces from the domain of religion. However, in keeping with our very human predilection for categorizing and organizing these phenomena, they continue to be assigned, not to some deity, but each to its own separate area of science. It is no longer the gods to whom we appeal for help or explanations, nor priests to whom we turn for advice, help, and guidance. Instead we look to climatologists, meteorologists, seismologists, oceanographers, medical researchers, and so forth, for explanation and for help in taming the hostile elements of nature. At the same time, philosophers and theologians seek answers to questions of morality and ethics, the origin of the universe and the epistemological questions that would seem to encompass all other questions. We continue to seek answers to aging and death in science and religion, where this seems inadequate. The ultimate questions on the origin of the universe, on the meaning and purpose of life and the nature of man's soul have not been neglected and though religion still offers answers, other explanations are now sought in science, mathematics, physics and in philosophy. But the questions and the fears remain:

> ... But the dread of something after death, /
> The undiscovered country from whose bourn/
> No traveler returns, puzzles the will/
> And makes us rather bear the ills we have/
> Than fly to those we know not of.
>
> (Shakespeare: Hamlet)

A general scientific and philosophical concept about the origins of the universe, time and space are today virtually common knowledge, but with this familiarity has come certain contempt for speculation on these fundamental questions. It has also produced widely varying explanations even within our own culture. Physicists and mathematicians offer complex mathematical constructs to explain the incomprehensible. At the same time philosophers dwell on aspects of being and time, but these abstractions of being and time, which we take for granted represent only the most recent conclusions in the long history of inquiry into the fundamental questions about the nature of existence. Yet, each small step along this road has meant a leap in the knowledge that had gone before it. The isolation of time as an aspect of the universe is in itself an ancient discovery; it is not immediately an apparent aspect of our universe. Rather, it is a true discovery and like most discoveries it took inquisitiveness, time, reason, and perseverance to find those answers we take for granted today. Like people all through time, the thinkers of the earliest Hindu tradition speculated on the origins of the universe, on being, man's mortality and on the survival of that vital force which departs the body when a man dies. Perhaps the greatest contribution of these ancient wise men was the tentative separation of deities from their culture, questions of the origin that exists and fate of man's vital life force. In the process they also introduced a far greater question, that of the incomprehensible nature of existence.

When we take on the task of discovering what unique Hindu ideas the Hindu *kavi* (seers/poets) have contributed in answering these questions, first we look at the body of knowledge that existed at even earlier stages in the development of Indian culture. In order to discover what is truly unique about Hindu origin as opposed to those ideas, which were inherited from the cultures of earlier times. In India the speculations on the ultimate questions of the origin of the world and the meaning of life surely dates back even beyond the time of the appearance of the Indo-European tribes in India which were the ancestors of the Hindus. The oldest records of Hindu thought that we find in the Vedic literature already reflect thoughts on the origins of the universe, time, man's mortality and ethics and the survival of the vital life force of the individual (what Western scholars have elected to translate with the narrowly Western concept of 'soul'). Though these thoughts represent perhaps only very modest steps when compared with today's inquiries, our perception is certainly clouded by the concepts originating from our own culture and our own bias in assessing the ideas from the past in other cultures. Still the speculations of the Hindus profoundly influenced the developing Indian culture, ultimately forming the basis for Indian religions. And - what is even more significant - the ideas originating in India have spread far beyond their birthplace to influence many other religions and philosophies of the world, ultimately giving new direction and impetus to speculations on these same questions in many other cultures. But a particularly significant development in thought which emerged in India in the course of these early speculations was a perception of man's existence in which the individual is measured against a vast and incomprehensible universe into which the life force of the individual is, in Hindu thought, ultimately absorbed.

Where and when did these ideas originate? How did they emerge from the body of ideas inherited from an earlier stage in the emerging Hindu culture? These ideas about the nature of the world in which we live, ideas which subsequently have become the determining factor in Hindu religion and have exerted profound influence on philosophical and theological thought in our own European civilization.

As speakers of English, we, like the members of every other culture, tend to take our language and culture for granted without inquiring into their origin or history, but the knowledge of the early stages of our language and its relationship to other languages and cultures in prehistoric times opens up for us the possibility of examining and comparing the development of basic ideas and concepts which, among other things, are the focus of this discussion. When we look for the origin of our own ideas in western civilization in trying to answer the fundamental questions about man's existence, we ultimately discover in the remote past some contact with Hindu thought - and, too, with the origin of similar ideas in other language families related to the language of the Hindu. Limited as our information may be, it still provides insight even into the common Indo-European thought.

The remoter roots of English and Sanskrit are to be found in the language which is their common source, i.e., from the "Indo-European" parent language, which flourished in east central Europe, possibly around 3500 B.C.

Some may have argued that it originated on the plains north of the Black Sea, or in the Danube valley, or in the region to the south of the Baltic Sea. The oldest known group to branch off was the Hittites, who migrated into Asia Minor, leaving "Indo-European" behind sometime around 2500 B.C. A few hundred years later, another migration of yet an additional contingent from this same '*urheimat*' penetrated into what is present-day Iran and northern India. This group of wanderers ultimately became what is known as the Indo-Iranian branch of the Indo-European family of languages. In their new home they developed their own unique culture and it was here that the new religion of the Hindus sprang up. The sacred literature of these people has not been passed down to us in written form; instead it has survived to this day in an oral tradition. This providing us with the spoken language of a remote time and place as well as some limited insight into the culture and - most importantly - into the thought of these people who had ventured boldly into new lands, and into whole new areas of intellectual speculation. From their ancient home they had brought with them concepts about nature, the universe and the moral and religious attitudes of their parent culture. To these, the Hindus added their own new *devas* - the name which they used to designate the anthropomorphized forces of nature and of moral and ethical principles, and out of this emerged the innovative speculations inspired by the ancient concepts. In the course of their questioning, arose the profound ideas, which have since come to be characterize by the body of Indian thought for the rest of the world.

But what were these ideas? How did the Hindu thinkers find the particular route they chose in developing their thought on the questions of being and time, the origin of the world, life and death, and on man's destiny? The goal of this study is to delineate these specific ideas and to explore their sources in the history of Hindu thought. The first question is:

PART I

HOW MUCH OF HINDU THOUGHT WAS IMPORTED FROM THE INDO-EUROPEAN SOURCE LANGUAGE?

The migrations of the Indo-European tribes continued throughout several millennia. The group, which was to become the source for Greece, moved from their *urheimat,* journeying south into the areas of what was to become Greece. During the course of their expansion, the Minoan civilization absorbed languages. From the north in the regions of present day northern Germany came the Italic branch of the Indo-European language family that migrated into the regions of central Italy, overrunning the indigenous populations and giving birth to the 'grandeur that was Rome.' The Celtic speakers expanded from regions around present day Netherlands and Belgium, eventually spreading out across all of Europe as far as the Black Sea in the East, regions of France and Spain in the west and in the north crossing the channel into the British Isles and Ireland. The Balto-Slavic group did not travel far from its original homeland and the Germanic elements - among which were the forbearers of English, German, Dutch, Swedish, Danish, Norwegian, etc., remained for a long time in what appears to have been their original homeland.

Within these language families, the essential features of the original Indo-European language survived along with the substantial traces of the shared cultures of the Indo-European people. From the shared lexicon which historical linguists have been able to reconstruct we are able to derive some notion of the daily life of these peoples, their culture, and their 'Weltanschauung'. It is striking that, even though each of the emerging language groups knows its own pantheon of gods who rule over all aspects of life, there are very few shared gods, if indeed there are any, which have survived from this earliest period. The one most prominent and most universally shared deity is the god - if, indeed, we are even correct in calling this a god - whose very appellation, a two syllable noun, stands apart in the source language. This is the god who is known in Hindu as 'Dyaus' or, as invoked in solemn ceremonies '*Dyāušpitar*' = 'heaven father' (*dyāuš* + *pitar* 'father') in the form of a vocative, i.e., a summoning of this god. This same appellation occurs in several of the Indo-European language families indicating that it originated at a time long before the division into the separate languages of later times[1]. Thus Greek *Zeus* (Ζεύς from **dyāús*) is the equivalent of Sanskrit *Dyāuš* and Greek *Zeu pater* (Ζεῦ πάτερ), the equivalent of the Sanskrit vocative. Latin also knows this deity in much the same forms, though somewhat more 'frozen', thus *Juppiter*/*Jū-piter* is the equivalent of the Sanskrit appellation *Dyāušpitar* while the genitive case of this same noun drops the vocative form and becomes simply *Jovis*. This Indo-European word is derived from a simpler word root **dei-*, with it variants *deye-*, *dī-*, and *dyā-* which had the basic meaning 'brightly shining, glittering, radiant',

[1]The etymologies here come from J. Pokorny's *Indogermanisches Etymologisches WÖrterbuch*, Bern & München: Francke Verlag. 1969.

e.g., the Sanskrit *didēti* 'shines', Old Norse[2] *teitr* 'cheerful, happy', Greek (Homeric) δέατο 'appeared', and many more.

The source for the Indo-European word from which the Sanskrit *Dyauš* derived, is also the source of the word which we find in Latin *diēs* 'day.' In striking parallel to the appellation for the god *Juppiter/Jū-piter*, Latin also shows the form *Diēspiter*, i.e., precisely the same form, but with the Latin word for 'day'. The use of this root in the sense of 'day' is found in several other Indo-European languages, e.g., Old Irish *dīe* 'day'; Sanskrit *divā* 'by day', *divēdivē* 'daily', and also as a noun *divam* 'heaven, sky'.

From the various possible vowel gradations of the basic Indo-European root we find a number of words in the general sense of 'sky, heaven' or 'god', e.g., from the Indo-European form **diwios*: Sanskrit *divya-* 'heavenly', which corresponds to Latin *dīus* 'divine', Greek δῖος 'divine'. And from the vowel grade **dyu-* we have Sanskrit *dyu-mnam* 'glory of the sky', cf. Russian *dožd'* 'rain'.

The vowel grade *deiwo-* was particularly productive: Sanskrit *dēva-* 'god (the heavenly being)'; Avestan *daēva* 'demon'; Oscan *deívaí* 'goddess'; Latin *dīves* 'wealthy', *deus/dīvus* 'deus'; Gallic (personal name) *Dēvognāta*, Old Irish *dia* 'god', Welsh *duiu* (*-tit*) 'god (-head)'. Here, too, belongs the name of the Germanic god known in Old English as *Tíw,* preserved in modern English in the name of the day of the week 'Tuesday', in Old Norse it is known as *Týr* and in Old High German as *Zīw*. But what was originally in Indo-European the appellation of the supreme god has become, in the Germanic language family,

---

[2]The Old Norse etymologies are taken from J. de Fries, *Altnordisches Etymologisches Wörterbuch*, Leiden: E. J. Brill, 1962.

the name of just one of the many gods of the Germanic pantheon. However, the plural form of the Indo-European noun remains as the name for the plural 'gods', in Old Norse *tīvar* 'gods'.

This is far from a complete inventory of the use of this appellation in the Indo-European language families; there are still other forms of the noun, which are used in the vocabulary of rites and ceremonies. The Indo-European noun is unusual in that it appears to derive from a root with two syllables while most Indo-European roots are limited to one syllable only. The basic form would look something like this: **dei-w-* and this root would have been attached to various stems forming endings with accompanying variations in the basic form of the root. Thus Sanskrit *devas* 'heavenly being' is derived from a form of the root **deiwo-* which corresponds to Latin *dīvus*.

Within the individual language families of the larger Indo-European family we find whole legions of gods and in these 'lesser' gods we see the personification of forces of nature, social norms, and man's own passions in war, in creative fervor, passion, and in amour. The Indo-European **dēiwos* stands apart from these in that it does not appear to be the personification of some natural phenomenon, but rather the phenomenon itself which was the object of veneration. The widely attested and clearly original Indo-European form, which appears as Vedic *Dyāušpitā* clearly anthropomorphizes the phenomenon with the added 'father'. This is reminiscent of the Old Norse appellation *Alfaðr* for the Scandinavian *Oðinn.* Though one must not conclude from this ultimate phenomenon was held to be the unique source of all that exists, even though *Dyāušpitā* may not have been the one and only god, some notion of monotheism is implicit in the concept of a unique source for all that exists. However, subtle idea might be ultimately provide the basis for a monotheistic interpretation of the origin of the world and all that is in it.

A sample of older pantheons of some of the related Indo-European languages in comparison with the earliest of the Hindu *devas* demonstrates the innovation in the realm of the religious cults characteristic of the individual language families. This will help in closely defining what part of the Hindu pantheon is inherited from the parent language, culture and creation of the Indian culture. E. O. James[3] sees in the deva inherited from the Indo-European mother language and the Hindus devas, that was a struggle between the Indo-European sky god, i.e., *Dyāuš*, and the gods of the indigenous population.

The Hindu *devas*[4]:

- **Indra**: from the Indo-European root **oid-* 'swell', *oidos 'swelling'. This root is attested in several languages, e.g., Greek οἰδέω 'I swell', οἶδος 'swelling'; and in the Germanic languages: Old High German *eiz*, noun, 'boil, and infected sore'. From this meaning in the Germanic languages comes the extended sense of 'poisonous secretion' and thus Old High German *eitar*, Old English *ātar*, Old Norse *eitr* 'pus'. The name of the Hindu deva *Indra-* comes from Sanskrit *indra-* 'strong' and occurs also in the name of the Avestan god *Indra-*. As the name of a god this root is known only in the Indo-Iranian language family.

---

[3]E. O. James. Myth and Ritual in the Ancient Near East. London: Thames and Hudson. 1963.

[4]Etymologies for Sanskrit words are based in part on Pokorny (see above) and on Manfred Mayrhofer. *Kurzgefasstes etymologisches W örterbuch des Altindischen: a concise etymological Sanskrit dictionary.* Heidelberg: C. Winter, 1956ff.

- **Agni**: Sanskrit *agnis* 'fire', *Agnis* 'name of a deva'; otherwise, only as the designation for fire: Latin *ignis,* Lithuanian *ugnís,* Old Bulgarian *ognъ* etc. Agni was counted the chief priest among the gods and a hymn to this *deva* opens the *Rig Veda.* It is Agni, after all, who 'goes among the devas' as it says in this hymn because it is Agni = fire who bears the offerings aloft to the devas and makes the connection between deva and man.
- **Mitra**: Sanskrit *mitra-* 'friend (from the Indo-European root **mei-* 'bind'); Avestan *miθra-* 'friend'. Sanskrit *Mitra-* 'name of a deva', Avestan *miθra* 'name of a deva'. Otherwise the Indo-European root shows only the meaning of 'bind', c.f. Greek μίτρη 'girdle, headband'.
- **Varuna;** as with so many of the names of devas in Hindu this does not lack in possible explanations, but a derivation which would connect it indisputably to some specific root is lacking as, too, is any outside correlate which might aid in fixing the true origin. According to the renowned indologist Paul Thieme *Varuna* is derived from the Hindu root *var-*, Indo-European **ver-* 'speak' in the meaning 'true/truth.' This seems particularly justified because *Varuna* is in the *Rig Veda* the heavenly deva, the most prominent of the devas, he who watches over justice and particularly over oaths. Wolfgang Meid, however, would derive this from Sanskrit. *vrnoti* 'surround, protect', *varutar-* 'protector, defender', *Varuna-* would then have the general sense of 'one who binds, joins together'. There are no other Indo-European names of gods formed from this particular root; it is a uniquely Hindu name.
- **Shiva**: This, too, is a uniquely Hindu name and even its origin is unclear. Some scholars associate this with the Sanskrit word *šēva-*, adjective, 'friendly, dear, precious', *šiva-* adjective 'dear, salubrious'. Beyond Sanskrit only in such words as Latin *civis* 'citizen', Oscan *ceus* 'id.'

Gothic heiwa-frauja 'householder', Old English *hīwan* 'housemate, family', Latvian Siva 'woman, wife'.

- **Manu**: This probably belongs to the Indo-European root **men-* /*mon- 'think'; examples from this root are numerous and are to be found in virtually every Indo-European language, e.g., Sanskrit *manyate 'thinks', manas* 'sense', *matis* (from *m-ti-) 'thought, opinion'; Avestan *mainyeite* 'thinks', *-maiti-* (in compound words) 'thought, opinion'; Greek *μέμονα* 'think about, desire to', and similarly Latin *meminī* 'recall, think about'; Old Norse *muna* ' think about, recall', Old English *mon*, *man* 'think about'. The name of the god is formed from this root with the stem forming *-u-* (not unlike the Indo-European *deiu-* from which Sanskrit *Dyāuš*). The same form is to be found in the Germanic languages in the word for *man* and the name of the deva *Manu* (see below). The two names (Germanic *Manu* and Sanskrit *Manu*), similar though they are, seem to have developed independent of each other, i.e., they do not appear to have been derived from a common name for this god.
- **Vishnu**: Another uniquely Sanskrit name with many potential derivations, but lacking any satisfactory explanation of its origin. The more widely accepted explanation derives this name from the Sanskrit root *vī-* 'to go apart in different directions' and *sānu* - 'ridge, peak', in the meaning 'who has spread out over the earth's peaks, etc.'.
- **Brahman**: According to Paul Thieme this is derived from the Sanskrit word *brahman-* 'forming, shaping', Middle Iranian *brahm* 'form, phenomenon'; possibly also in this group is the Old Norse word *bragr* 'poetry', all from the Indo-European root *bheregh-* 'high'. Also suggested as a possible source is Indo-European *bhlagh-* 'flame', though this seems a far less likely source.

- **Uṣās**: from: **us-*; Indo-European *awes- / aus- / wes- / us-* , 'daybreak, dawn'); Greek *ἠώς* from: **āusōs*; Latin *aurōra* from: **āusōsā*)'sunrise'.
- **Yama**: Deva of the realm of the dead, Skrt. *yama-* "twin." <IE. **yemo* "twin, hermaphrodite"; c.f. Germanic, Old Norse *Ymir* the primordial giant from whose body man emerges and the world is created; <Germ. **yumyiaz*
- **Kali**: Feminine noun of the adj *kala-* 'black', i.e., 'the black one'. *Kali* is often seen in combination with *Yama* in the realm of the dead. Kali is one aspect of *Durga*, the mate of *Shiva,* who appears in this form as the terrifying challenger of demons. In early times her menacing side was propitiated with human sacrifice. On her 'good' side Durga is venerated as the kindly mother who brings food to living creatures.

Figure 1: Yama is pictured in this frieze (smaller figure upper center of the frieze with Kali (lower center). From: Asian Museum of Art; San Francisco)

The names of the Indian devas Mitra, Varuna, and Indra as well as the pair Nāsatya (=not na+asatya, i.e. not deceitful = Ašvins the pair of charioteers who arrive with the dawn in their golden horse-drawn chariot), sun gods are found in a Hittite inscription describing a treaty (ca. 1400 BC) between the Hittite king Suppiluliumas and Mattinaza the ruler of the Mitanni.[5] The names are clearly of Sanskrit

[5]E. O. James, The Worship of the Sky God. Lonton: Anthlone Press. University of London 1963, speculates that the gods named in this treaty are of Indian origin. The evidence presented here certainly gives credence to this speculation and also indicates that these Hindu devas are unique to the Hindu

origin and thus indicate that the deities of the Mitanni, which are also of Sanskrit origin. This evidence for the presence of speakers of the early Sanskrit language in this region is also found in the Hittite language where a number of terms used in horse training are also clearly drawn from Sanskrit.
Thus:

aikawartanna 'simple turn'
tērawartanna 'triple turn'
panzawartanna 'quintuple turn'
šattawartanna 'septuple turn'
nāwartanna 'ninefold turn'

The term for the simple turn (*aikawartanna*) makes the Sanskrit origin of the word particularly clear. The element *aika-* = Sanskrit *eka-* 'one' is unique among the Indo-European languages in that the usual form for this word is Indo-European *oino-* as in Gothic (a Germanic language) *ains* 'one' or Greek οἶνος 'the number *one* on a die', Sanskrit *ēna-* 'he', Latin *ūnus*, from Old Latin *oino,* and many more such forms from other Indo-European language groups. The Sanskrit form with its -ka- suffix stands alone in its form among all the related Indo-European languages and clearly marks the recorded Mitanni form as Sanskrit in origin.

Each of the Indian devas is associated with some specific area of activity and ritual in which the particular deva is invoked, this is this activity which the priest wishes to 'activate'. Indra, for example, is the mighty deva, the slayer of the serpent that holds the waters captive in his

---

religion and not borrowed from some other culture.

mountain lair. In invoking Indra, with his 'club-arm', the flashing lightning bolt, Indra slays the serpent and frees the captive waters.

The Greek gods[6]**:**

- **Apollo**[7]**:** 'Απόλλων; Illyrian personal names such as *Mag-aplinus*, *Aplus*, *Aplo*, etc.; Gallic *Dī-ablintes* (from **aplentes*); Germanic names of female gods (in Latin inscriptions): *Matronis Aflimms* (dative plural), *Afliabus* 'who work magic', Old Norse *afol*, Old English *afol*, *abal* 'strength'.
- **Ares** ῎Αρης, 'god of vengeance', the personification of Greek ἀρή 'ruin, act of violence' with no cognates beyond the Greek god.
- **Aphrodite**: Goddess of love, daughter of Zeus and Dioné. The name has no cognates beyond the Greek; from Greek ἀφρός 'foam', 'born of foam'.
- **Dionysos** Διόνυσος= **Bacchus** (Βάκχος): Dionysos, which occurs only in Greek.
- **Demeter**: Δημήτηρ, cf. Doric Δᾶμᾱτηρ (from the Indo-European root **gđhō-* 'earth'), with the initial syllable modeled on Demeter's cognomen Δαμία.
- **Artemis**: ρτεμις (from ἀρτεμῆς which in turn derives from *ἀρτι- + δεμής - from δέμας i.e., *arti-* 'correct' + *demas* 'body', 'whose body is well formed'.
- **Atlas**: τλας (gen. τλαντος); from Greek ταλάςςαι,

[6]Information on the etymological sources for the Greek names is taken in part from H. G. Lidell & R. Scott. *A Greek - English Lexicon*. New York: American Book Company. 1897, and from R. Schmitt. *Dichtung und Dichtersprache in indogermanischer Zeit.* Wiesbaden: Otto Harossowitz, 1967, and, far more general and less reliable: Leeming, D. A. & Leeming, M. A. *Encyclopedia of Creation Myths*. Santa Barbara: ABC-CLIO, 1994.

[7]For further information of the Greek gods see: Long, Charlotte R. The Twelve Gods of Greece and Rome. Leiden : E. J. Brill.1987

'bear, suffer', present participle τλάς "Now Iapetus took to wife the neat-ankled maid Clymene, daughter of Ocean, and went up with her into one bed. And she bore him a stout-hearted son, Atlas."

- **Titans**: These are the children of Uranus, the earliest supreme god who is a personification of the sky; Uranus was the son and also the consort of Gaea, the goddess of the earth who also produced the Cyclopes - and Titans.
- **Athena**: ɔΑθήνη from Greek ἄνθος; IE *andh-, n̥dh-, Greek ἄνθος 'flower', ἀνθέω 'I flower'; Sanskrit *and-has* 'the soma plant', *adhvan* = Avestan *advan* 'way, path', *adhvaras* 'religious ceremony'.
- **Hermes**: ῾Ερμῆς, with no immediate cognates beyond Greek.
- **Hera**: ῾Ηρα from Indo-Germanic **ser-* 'protect, guard', Avestan *haraiti* 'take care, protect.'

Roman gods:

Beyond the already mentioned god, Latin Jup(p)iter, there are very few Roman gods who are clearly of an exclusively Roman origin. The influence on Roman civilization from Greece is strong and Greek gods often became the models for Rome. Their function is defined by the Greek models and does not reflect the original significance of the god or his origin.

- **Venus**: from the Indo-European root **wen-* 'love, desire, contentment'; Sanskrit *vanati*, *vanoti* 'desires, loves, gains, conquers'; Old Norse *vinr* 'friend, Old Saxon / Old High German *wini,* Old English *wine* 'friend', and many more.
- **Diana**: This is yet another derivative of the root *dyēus*, in this instance with the form **diwio-*; the original form of this particular word was **Diviāna*, possibly in the

meaning 'belonging to the goddess of the dawn **Diviā* '.

- **Minerva**: According to C. Lewis and C. Short. *A Latin Dictionary*. Oxford: At the Clarendon Press. 1969, this is from the Indo-Germanic root **men-* 'think' as in the Germanic word for *man*, etc. Minerva is the goddess of wisdom, arts and sciences, etc. after the model of Pallas Athena.
- **Ceres**: Goddess of the fruit-bearing earth, of Indo-Germanic **ker-* 'grow, cause to grow'; Greek κόρος 'satiety', κορέσω 'satiate'; Latin *crēscō* 'grow', etc.
- **Jūno**: daughter of Saturn, wife and sister of Jupiter. No clear cognates beyond Latin.
- **Mars**: According to C. Lewis and C. Short, ibid. This is from the Indo-European root **(s)mer-*,as in Sanskrit *smarati* 'remember, think of', Lat. *memor* 'think of'; Old Norse *Mímir* 'name of a giant', Old English *mimorian* 'remember'., etc.

To these divinities the Romans eagerly (Latter half of the first millennium BC) began to add an almost endless number of minor divinities or divine forces to explain/help deal with routine occurrences. This applied both to the objects and to the events which played a role in daily living and could include events such as the phases of the moon, the seasons of the year, the motions of the planets, actions of volcanoes, storms, etc. They could also incorporate objects from the implements used in agriculture, war, household tools, burial sites, the 'ghosts', which are to be found in the home, the hearth, and so on. To these many deified functions of daily life the Romans gave the name *numen* n. 'sign of divine will, etc.' from the Latin verb *nuō* as in *renuō* 'to deny - with a nod of the head.'

The spirits of the dead, the *Manes*, also continued to influence the actions of the living while the *genius loci,* the guardian spirit of a place, exercised its influence in the specific location.

The Germanic gods[8]:

The Germanic gods are of particular interest for us because the languages of this northern European region seem to have undergone a much more conservative evolution and preserve many features of the Indo-European mother language for us. The Mediterranean languages on the other hand, were constantly exposed to alien influences, which seem to account for the earlier and more rapid rate of language change.

- **God**: this first of the Germanic names for deities is a uniquely Germanic creation. Germanic *guða-*; Old Norse *guð*, Old English *god*, Old Saxon *god*, Old High German *got*, Gothic *guþ*. The Indo-European source seems to be *ghu-to m* from the root *gheu-* as in Sanskrit *hū-* "invoke the gods." The word would have originally referred to the invocation of some deity and then to the *thing* or *deity* being invoked." The word is, in the Germanic languages, a neuter noun and did not refer to a personified deity but rather to an invoked force.
- ***Þunaraz:** (The * indicates a historically reconstructed word.) the Germanic thunder god; Old English *Þunor*, Old Saxon *Thuner*, Old Norse *Þórr*, Old High German *Donar*: a common Germanic deity who enjoyed wide spread popularity among the Germanic peoples. In the translation of the Latin days of the week into the Germanic languages - which occurred quite early in the history of the contact between these two important language groups - Þórr took the place of Juppiter, Latin:

[8]The Germanic etymologies are taken from J. de Fries (see above); Kluge, F. Etymologisches Wörterbuch der deutschen Sprache. Bearb. Von Mitzka, W., Berlin: Walter de Gruyter, 1960; Schmitt, R. (see above).

Jovis dies, as **Þonaresdag* "Thursday." For the analysis of the roles of the Germanic gods which assume some fundamental identity between the gods of the Indo-Germanic peoples, however, this is an example of the fallacy of such broad determinations; since aside from the brandishing of the thunderbolt the two have very little else in common. Þórr resembles more the Roman god Hercules in his primitive behavior and great physical strength, his heavy drinking and voracious appetite. He is also the god who undertakes journeys to fight against evil creatures and is the friend of the common man, Old Norse *vinr verliða*. With his hammer he recalls to us the Greek *Heros* or the Hindu god *Indra*. **þórr** is thus most frequently compared with Hercules in the Germanic traditions. Tacitus speaks of a Germanic *silva Herculi sacra,* i.e., a "forest sacred to Hercules" by which is meant the Germanic god *Þórr.* In the region of the Germanic tribe of the Batavians in Northern Germany, numerous inscriptions dedicated to *Hercules Magusānus* have been found and in *Noviomagus*, the Latin form of the Older (originally Celtic) name which is today the Dutch City of Nijmagen.

- ***Tīw**- was a god who the Romans glossed either as Mars or Mercury. According to Tacitus, the Germanic tribe of the Tencturians worshiped this god above all others, but this was quite probably only in times of battle. This god is, in his name, the actual chief of the Indo-European gods (see above) and is well attested in virtually all of the related languages. In earlier Germanic times *Tīw-* was still worshipped as the primary god only among the *Swebi* (Swabians) in Southern Germany. The Indo-European god was in all Germanic languages only a war-god and in the translation of the week-days **Tīw-* (Old Norse *Týr*, Old English *Tíw* / *Tíg* Old High German *Zīo*) takes the place of Mars - *dies Martis* = Old Norse *Týsdagr*, Old English *Tíwesdæg*. Among the Saxons his god was known also as Old Saxon *Saxnōt*, Old English *Seaxnéat*.

- Old Norse **Óðinn**, Germanic ***Wōdanaz** literally "lord of the raging horde = *wōda-*", the word formation following Gothic *Þiudans* "king, lord of the *þiuda* = people" from the Germanic/Gothic *wōþs* "raging, possessed (e.g., by demons)"; c.f. Latin vātes Gallish οὐάτεις (wateis) "seer." Wodan is, then, the leader of the possessed, mad crowd. His name takes the place of that of Mercurii in the names of the weekdays: Old English *Wōdnesdœg*, Old Norse *Óðinsdagr*. This name is absent from the German calendar where it is replaced by *Mittwoch* imitating Greek *media hebdomas* in its formation and avoiding the name of what was apparently a particularly offensive (to Roman and Christian observers) Germanic deity. According to Adam of Breman... *Wodan, id est furor, bella gerit homine, ministrat virtutem contra inimicos*; and: Paulus diaconis 1,9... *Wotan sane... ipse est qui apud Romanos Mercurius dicitur.*
- ***frijjō**: The only female deity in the common Germanic pantheon is Old Norse *Frigg*, Old English *Fríg*, Old Saxon *Frīg*, Old High German *Frīja* "wife of Wodan". Old Norse *frjádagr* "Friday", Old English *frígedœg*, Old High German *frīatag* translate Latin *dies Veneris*. The name derives from a common Germanic root found in Old English *frēon* "to love", Old Norse *frjá* id, Gothic frijōn id. The Indo-European root for this word is found in Sanskrit *priya-* "dear, beloved", *prīyate* 'loves', etc. The Old Norse form comes from a Germanic form of the name *frijjō. The name Freyja is from the same root as OHG. *frouwa* 'lady, noble woman'; OE. frúa id., MLG. vrouwe id. These are feminine forms of the Germanic word, which occurs in ON. *Freyr*, Gothic *frauja* 'lord, master'. These come from an Indo-European root *prwo-, Skrt. *pūrvya* '(the) first'.

From the Germanic deities mentioned by the Roman historian Tacitus we have several additional gods of significance in the comparison of the Indo-European divinities:

- **Tuisto**: Old Saxon *twisc*, Old High German zwisc "twice, twin". C.f. OE. *twist* "twice folded, i.e. yarn." It is generally agreed that the name means something like "hermaphrodite" which would account for the ability of this deity to produce progeny without the aid of a second being (the related Sanskrit *Yama* means "twin" and makes this meaning quite possible here). There seems to be a similarity here with the god Burí who was born out of the primordial ice -- licked free by the great cow.
- **Mannu**: OE. *monn*, ON. *maðr* (<*mannr*), OS. & OHG. *man(n)* from IE. **men* / **mon*, *mn-* "think". Man is the thinking being: Skt. *mánu- mánus-* and the god *Manu* (the laws of Manu, etc.).
- **Ing**: OE. *Ing*, ON. *Yngvi*, Gothic *Enguz* (actually **Iggus* or **iggws*). In Cheruscian proper name, *Inguiomerus* "Ing-famed"; Beowulf: proper name *Ingwine* "Ing friends", said of the Danes. *Yngvi* / *Ingvi* / *Yngvifreyr* / *Ingvifreyr* / *Ynglingar*: Gothic rune name *enguz*, c.f. Tocharian A *onk*, B *enkwe* "man." The Germanic form of the name of this god would have been: **Ingwaz*, Ole English *Ing* and from this Germanic form comes the form *Yngvi* "Ingwion", and the other related forms: *Yngvifreyr* "lord of the Ingwions", *Ynglingar* "descendant of the *Ingwions*." *Ing* was a fertility god as figurines depicting him clearly show.

There are of course, many more divine forces, which the Germanic peoples acknowledged as gods. In his *Prose Edda* Snorri Sturlasson lists a number of gods not known to us from any other source, scholars have been inclined to attribute these to Snorri's inventive genius. But when we see how the Romans expanded the vast ranks of divine forces whose will impinges on human activities, it does not seem at all unlikely that the Germanic people - including the Norse tribes - had gone through a very similar process. The Old High German magic formula called the Mereseburger Zauberspruch mentions the goddesses *Volla*, *Sunna*, and *Sinthgunt*, who are not known to us from any other sources. To divinities such as these we may also add the many locations - mountains, streams, forests, and sacred sites, to which attach divine forces.

Summarizing the Indo-European Divinities Common to all the language families

This catalogue of sources for the names of gods of some of the major cultures of the Indo-European language family is certainly nowhere near complete. The number of gods in each individual language group is great and it would be a major task just to discover all of the gods in each of the groups touched on here. The object of this review, however, has been to discover few examples through what has survived from this Indo-Germanic 'Urzeit' into the individual language groups. It seems clear from these etymologies that beyond the one supreme Indo-European god whose name survives in Hindu *Dyāus,* there is virtually no other god from this earlier period that has made it into the history of various cultures. This suggests that the speakers of the source language may not have had any great number of specific gods beyond this one 'sky' god. The derivation of the words for gods from the individual languages e.g., nouns such as Sanskrit *devas*, *divas*, Greek *dios*, Latin *divus*, *dīvus*, *deus*, Germanic - Old English *tīw*, etc., all derived from this one older name, suggests that the pantheon of subordinated gods which we find in the individual languages had somehow been attached to this one god, but subordinated to this one fundamental concept. We might infer from this that the original view of the world was virtually monotheistic, but this would lead us far beyond what the actual information permits us to assume. It would also seem to be in contradiction to what we have always believed by observing other cultures. Importantly, though, in its focus on one apparently supreme god it does open the way for the development of the notion of one god as the source of all being.

Beyond the sample etymologies given above we do have a few additional bits of information about the cosmogony from the period before the emergence of the individual Indo-European languages. A number of agreements between the various Indo-European language families in the area of religious rites shows something of the beliefs which do survive into the later cultures emerging from the source language and culture. One of these is the striking phenomenon of the 'sun wheel'. This is an object that is described in the oldest Hindu texts, and is also found in Greek and in the Germanic language sources where it is widely attested[9] in religious texts and/or in graphical representations.

In Sanskrit texts we find:

Rig Veda, 1, 130, 9a: *sūraš čakra pra vrhajjāta ojasa* 'The sun's wheel he, born of strength, tore away'

Rig Veda 1,174, 5c: *prā sūraš čakra vrhatād abhīke* 'do not tear away the wheel of the closely approaching sun'

and:

[9] The following draws on R. Schmitt. Ibid.

Aeschylus; *Persi*: λαμπρὸς ἡλίου κύκλος 'the shining wheel of the sun' and Germanic:
Old Norse *Alvís mál*: 16,1 and 5: *sól heitir með mǫnnom álfar fagrahvél* 'among men ... [among] the elves the sun is called light-wheel'
Old Norse; *Harmsól* 36,7 *sunnu... hvél* 'sun's ... wheel'
Old English; *sunnan hweogal* 'sun's wheel'

In the domain of the Germanic tribes this curious usage is further encountered in the many petroglyphs, carvings, and other objects in which this sun wheel is actually depicted (v. illus.). The significance of this sun-wheel and its role in the religion of the particular cultures remains obscure, but its origin in the parent language and culture is assured. Certainly, there are a number of religions in which the sun is the center of some ritual, and the sky-god, which we find in Indo-Germanic **dēiwos* could have been the sun god as well. The origin of the name and its connection to the word for *day* and *light / bright* could in some way be at the bottom of this sun-wheel concept, but there is no substantiated link which would allow us to make this a valid claim.

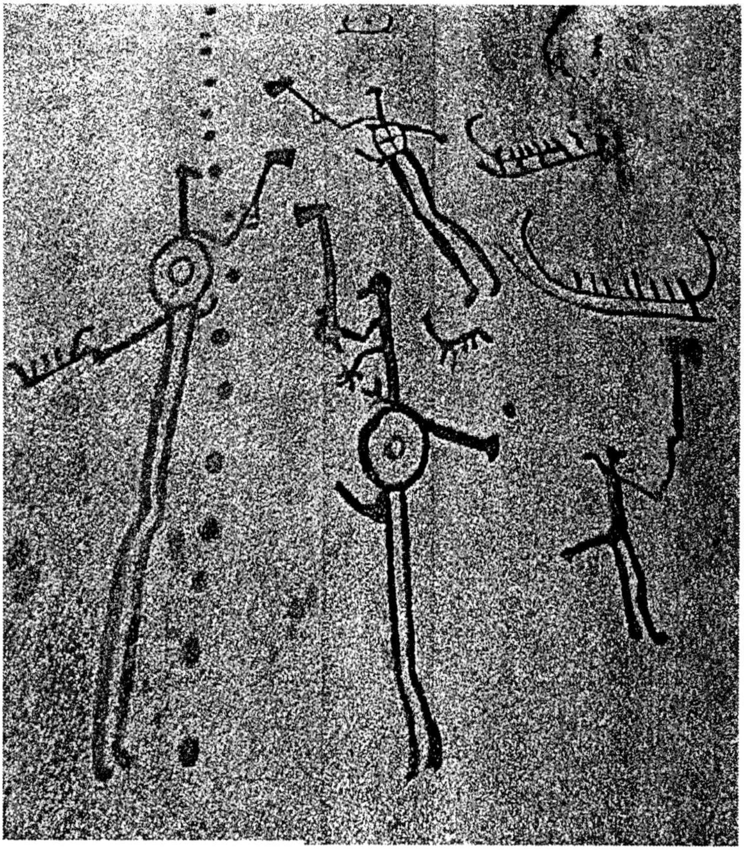

Figure 2: Notice the wheels in the center of the clearly male figures and the overly phalic character of the picture itself.
From: H. R. Ellis Davidson, *Scandinavian Myth* (New York: Paul Hamlyn, 1969)

In a somewhat similar vein we find in virtually all the Indo-Germanic language families the theme of the origin of the world out of the void or chaos. Again, this is an unusual phenomenon and we can conclude that it reflects a view of the world that goes back to the earliest times in the common Indo-Germanic period.

In the famous *Rig Veda* text, Book 10, 129, 3 we find:

> *darkness existed, in darkness concealed*
> *in the beginning, an invisible flood all this.*
> *whatever existed enclosed by void, this alone out of great heat (was) born.*

(The full text of this hymn with the translation follows in the next chapter)

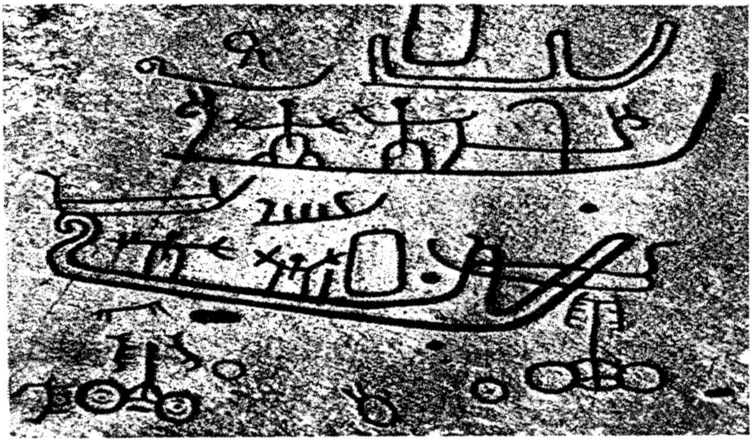

Figure 3: Aside from the wagon wheels (bottom left and right) there are still other wheel shapes between the two wagons in this petroglyph.
From: H. R. Ellis Davidson, *Scandinavian Myth* (New York: Paul Hamlyn, 1969)

Greek sources on the other hand have the world born out of the joining of Chaos with Gaea, the Earth-Mother. The name Chaos itself derives from the root found in Greek χάσκω 'yawn, gape'. The underlying Indo-European root is **ghē-* 'yawn, gape' with its variants **ghēi-*, **ghə-* and **ghī-*. From this same root come Latin *hiō*, *hiāre*''yawn, gape'; Old Norse *gína* Old English *tō-ginan* 'gape, yawn', and again from this root, but with the root variant *ghəbh-* we find Old Norse *gap* 'gap, wide opening', etc.

From the beginning stanzas of the Voluspa, the Old Norse poem in which the origin of the world is depicted, we hear:

3. *Ár var alda, þat er Ymir bygþi,*
vara sandr né sœr né svalar unir;
irþ fannz œva né upphiminn,
gap var ginnunga,enn gras hvergi.

It was the beginning of the ages when Ymir[10] *dwelt, there was neither sand nor sea nor cold waves.*
Nowhere was there earth nor heaven above. An abyss of chaos, nor was there any grass.

In this verse two different forms of the same Indo-European root **ghē-*, which occurs in Greek χάος is found in the final line. This is certainly not a compelling basis for suspecting a common Indo-European concept of a world born out of a primordial chaos. But among the great variety

[10] *Ymir*: the primordeal giant, <Germ. **yumyiaz* <IE. **yemo* "twin, hermaphrodite"; c.f. Skrt. *yama-* "twin."

of cosmologies in all cultures of the world only a few share this same vision. But even within the religions of the Indo-European language families there are significant inconsistencies in the descriptions of the origin of the world. The Germanic tradition as it appears in the Voluspa - and as it is supported by fragmented accounts from other regions of Germania such as the southern German Wessobrunner Gebet; for example, the emergence of the world *ex nihilo* is just one of many conflicting concurrent descriptions. In this same, Voluspa along side the above-cited stanza there are subsequent verses in which the world is described as being born out of an ice-filled chaos and assembled from the bones and body of the giant Ymir, the gods - whose origin is not explained, are doing all this labor. Thus, the apparent agreement found in the idea of a world born out of chaos does not prove an Indo-European source for the idea; still it does suggest something beyond the realm of chance. The possibility of a shared notion of some sort can not be excluded, even though this is not a concept limited exclusively to the Indo-European language families.

Similarly, in the hymns of the *Rig Veda*, which are the source for most of the descriptions of the early Hindu religion, we find several different versions in which the birth of the world seems to come out of nothingness or to be attributed to one or the other of the many Hindu *devas*. The text which raises the most penetrating questions about the origin of the world (RV 10, 129) is, in this regard, very different from the remaining hymns of the *Rig Veda*. This source is itself basically a collection (i.e., *Rig Veda sãhita* 'collection') of hymns from different '*kavi*' (wise men or poets) from different times and different geographical regions of India. In these hymns we see the product of an advanced, highly sophisticated tradition of poetry. The verse forms and metric varieties are diverse, yet very clearly defined, showing a large inventory of stanza forms with variations such as three and four line stanzas featuring characteristic eight, eleven, or twelve syllable lines. In turn these lines may show fixed metrical features such as the caesura following the fourth syllable in what is called the *gayatri* form. This tradition has its roots in Indo-European verse forms and we find parallel verse forms and even entire lines of verse repeated in other Indo-European languages. These include virtually identical lines of verse, which have occurred; for example, in Greek and Sanskrit. But it is important to stress that the Vedic poets have elaborated on the originals and produced in their own language, a body of poetry of unparalleled beauty and originality.

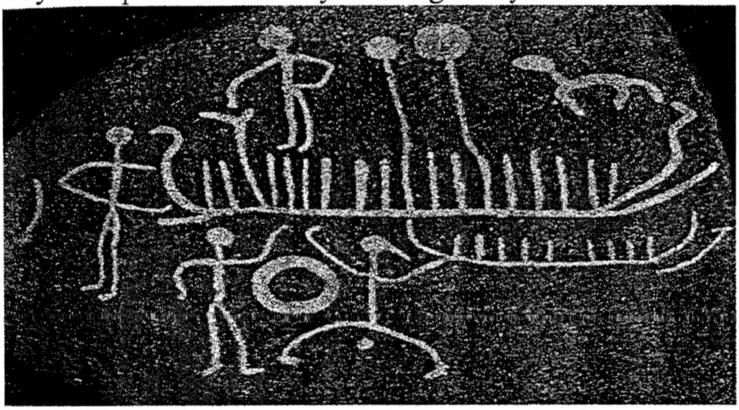

Figure 4: Note the wheel shapes above the ship and also below between two figures.
From: H. R. Ellis Davidson, *Scandinavian Myth* (New York: Paul Hamlyn, 1969)

The *Rig Veda* has generally been treated as an integral whole from which the basic tenants of the Hindu religion have been extracted. But such an interpretation of this text, as a fundamental *bible* is more in keeping with the Judeo-Christian tradition where the religion is based on one sacred text that is accepted as the infallible basis for religious doctrine. There is, for example, no single god whose deeds are to be praised, no unifying underlying concept of the goal of man's existence, no unique view on the origin of the world. E. O. James[11] has observed that: "In Vedic cosmology... there was no systematized cosmogony, or generally accepted conception of the origin, nature and content of the universe in its various forms, phases and manifestations." And, "The simplest interpretation of creation was that of the cosmic waters, ...in combination with the underlying primordial infinite space *Aditi*, the mother of the gods, in which natural phenomena, particularly the sky, the earth and the waters, were personified in a galaxy of gods and spirits." The hymns of the *Rig Veda* are the creation of poets passionately, enthusiastically, ecstatically singing the praises of particular devas. These cannot in any way be considered a collection of dispassionate, critical theological discussions of the profound questions and some of these *kavi*, the poet/seers who composed these works, do raise profound philosophical questions such as those we find in the 'creation hymn' of *Rig Veda* 10,129. In this particular hymn the kavi introduces the profound question of the origin of the world and the difficulties in discovering whether this is a creation of some *deva* or a spontaneous event or the consequence of the actions of some other yet to be identified source. In other hymns, however the kavi have

[11]E. O. James. Creation and Cosmology. Leiden: E. J. Brill. 1969.

touched on this question, but have in general tended to envision the world as the creation of some particular deva, devas or as having been put into order by one or the other deva, e.g., RV 2, 12 gl, ff. suggests a specific deva as the ordering force:

Yō jāta eva prathamo ma-
nasvān devo devan
kratunā pariyabhūšat
yasya ušmād rodasī ab-
hyasetā nrmasya mahnā
sa janāsa indra

He who was born first,
the wise deva, who served
the devas with (his)
strength, before whose
energy both worlds have
fear, the brave one, he, o
mortals, is Indra."

ya prthivī vyathamānām
adhad ya parvatān
prakupitā armāt
yo antarikša vimane
varīyo yo dyām astabhnāt
sa janasa indra

"He who made stable the
quivering world, who
makes the trembling
mountains stand still, who
has stridden farther
through the space be-
tween heaven and earth,
who supported the
heaven, he, o mortals, is
Indra."

In the strongly mystical, speculative hymn, *Rig Veda* 10, 5, found another *deva* designated 'first-born' and there is also a tentative step toward answering the question of the origin of being out of non-being (i.e., *sat* from *asat*):

eka samudro dharuṇ rayṇām
asmad dhrdo bhūrijanmā vi
caṣṭeṣ / ṣiṣakty ūdhar ṇiyor
upastha utsasya madhye ni

The unique sea, the treasure
bearing, the prolific, speaks
from our hearts.
It seeks the udder in the
womb of the two hidden ones;

hitam padã veh

placed in the middle of the source the trace of the bird.

Samānã nīa vrṣaṇo vasānān
sã jagmire mahiṣā arvatībhi/
ṛtaṣya padã kavayo ni pānti
guhā nāmāni dadhire parāi.

Together into the nest concealing themselves the rutting buffalo came together with the studs. / The seers watch over the traces of the sacrifice, in concealment they hide their highest forms.

tāyinī māyinī sa dadhāte
mitvā iu jajñatur vardha-
yantī / vivasya nābhi carato
dhruvasya kave cit tantum
manasā viyanta.

The two wise, pious ones joined together, having formed an infant they gave birth and nourished it. It is the naval of all that moves or is firm, and the seers (poets?) cutting through the thread by (their) mind(s).

rtaṣya hi vartanaya sujātam
išo vājāya pradiva sacante /
adhīvāsa rodasī vāvasāne
ghtair annair vāvdhāte
madhūnām.

The path of right (is) surely to the wellborn; sacrificial libations, food ever follow / heaven and earth donning a cloak, having grown with ghee and food and sweets.

ṣapta svasir arušīr vāvaāno
vidvān madhva uj jabhārā
de kam /
antar yeme antarikṣe purāja
ichan vavrim avidat
pūšaṇasya.

Seven sisters fire-red clothed the knowing one pulled from the sweetness, to see them / whom born long ago stopped in the air, seeking a hiding place he found that of Pushan.

ṣapta maryādā kavayas ta-

Seven marks the seers created; to one of these went the

takṣus
tāsām ekam id abhy ahuro
gāt / āyor ha skambha
upamasya nīe patha visarge
dharueṣu tasthau.

hemmed in one. / Āyu's pillar stands in the nest of the highest one on firm ground at the paths'ends.

Asac ca sac ca parame
vyoman dakṣasya janmann
aditer upasthe /
agnir ha na pra thamajā tasya
pūrva āšabha ca dhanu.

Both non-being and being (are) in the highest heaven at the birth of Dakša in the womb of the Aditi. / Agni, truly, is for us the first born of the right in the earliest time and the bull and the cow.

In yet another hymn of the *Rig Veda*, *Book 10, 72*, we find further advances into the realm of speculation on the basic elements of the creation. In this hymn we also see the notion of 'born first' being more thoroughly examined, even if in a somewhat back-handed fashion:

Devānā̃ nu vayã jānā̃ pra
vocāma vipanyayā
ukthesụ asyamānesụ ya
payād uttare yuge.

In awe we want to proclaim the birth of the devas, in hymns of praise which later generations might consider.

Brahmaṇas patir etā sa
karmāra ivādhamat,
devānā pūrvye yuge 'sata
sad ajājayata.

Brahmanaspati has assembled these like a smith. In the early time of the devas being was born of non-being.

devānā̃ yuge prathame
'sata sad ajāyata,
tad āṣā anv ajāyanta tad
uttānapadas* pari.

In the first period of the
devas being was born of
non-being; were born the
areas of the world, this of
the birthing mother.

bhūr jajña uttānapado
bhuva āšā ajāyanta,
adhiter dako ajāyata dakād
v aditi.

The earth came into being
from the birthing mother.
The Aditi were born of the
Daka, from the Daka the
Aditi.

aditir hy ajanišṭa dakṣa yā
duhitā tava,
tā devā anv ajāyanta
bhadrā amrtabandhavah.

Aditi, o Daka, was born as
your daughter. After her
the devas were born, the
immortality-joined.

yad devā adah salile
susārabdhā atišhata,
atrā vo nrtyatām iva tīvro
reṣur apāyata.

When you devas stood to-
gether closely assembled
in the primordial flood,
then from you, much like
one dancing, a thick dust
went out.

yad devā yatayo yathā
bhuvanāny apinvata,
atrāsamudra ā gūlham ā
sūryam ajabhartana.

As the devas like magi-
cians expanded the worlds
they brought the sun con-
cealed in the sea.

aštau putrāso aditer ye
jātās tanvas pari,
devā upa prait saptabhi
parā mārtāṇam āsyat.

They are eight sons of the
Aditi who were born of her
body. To the devas seven
went, they pushed aside

	the martanda.
Saptabhih putrair aditir upa prait pūrvya yugam, prajāyai mrtyave tvat punar mārtāam ābharat.	With seven sons the Aditi went into the first age. They brought the martanda again so that he would propagate himself and then die.

* In the notes to his translation of this hymn Geldner[12] sees this phrase"... mit emporgestreckten Füssen..." as a position which in this context "weist eher auf eine eigentümliche Stellung der Gebärenden hin." i.e., it refers to a characteristic positioning of the body of the birthing mother.

The *Aditi* here are the female creation forces, the *Daka* the male, the necessary forces for the procreative act, which would have produced the world. Unlike the hymns such as that to Indra, *RV 2, 12* cited above, this is not an exuberant praise of the many accomplishments and virtues of a particular deva, but a search for the more basic questions, e.g., the origin of the devas and the birth of being out of non-being. It does not offer a coherent, well-conceived investigation into the questions, but provides an initial step in the search for answers to the ultimate questions, which are finally taken up in *RV 10, 129* where we find a far more coherent inventory of the questions and a catalogue of the potential answers. It is from this direction of inquiry that the questions arise, which has occupied later Hindu thinkers even to this day.

Among the many hymns of the *Rig Veda* we find several in which the creation of the world seems to be attributed to one or the other of the several Hindu *devas* or, as

[12] Geldner, Karl Friedrich. *Der Rig Veda*, vol III. The Harvard Oriental Series. Vol 45. Cambridge, MA: The Harvard University Press. 1951.

in *Rig Veda* 10, 90, out of the primordial being, *purusha*, much like the Germanic *Ymir*. These in turn have been the sources of the divergent directions, which Hinduism has taken in different areas of India. This divergency has led some scholars to search in the *Rig Veda* for the one, the true *deva* who created the world; for example, in the collection of essays by F. B. J. Kuiper presented by John Irwin in his book on ancient Indian cosmogony[13]. The research here appears to view the hymns as representative of a sort of unified whole, not unlike many interpretations of the Christian bible, the Koran, or the Talmud. There is a profound difference between the notion either of a world created out of nothing or out of some pre-existing element and the *spontaneous generation* of the world out of nothing. The search for the *deva* who created the world out of *asat* (non-being) has the same problem as that confronted by the kavi who composed RV 10, 129, wonders how there could be a *creation* or *origin* out of nothing. The *Rig Veda* does not give a consistent version of the nature of the *devas,* of the creation of the world, nor is such an explanation from the Rig Veda collection possible.

For the purposes of this study, in which we are searching for the origin of the concepts of time and being in Hindu philosophy, I have chosen to focus on one particular aspect of the Hindu philosophy, i.e., the origin of the awareness of the dilemma in the origin of the *devas* in the oldest Hindu philosophy. This gives rise to a particular direction in later Hindu thought and quite probably extends to similar directions in the philosophical speculation in the Near East.

---

[13]Irwin, John. *Ancient Indian Cosmogony*. Sahibabad: Vicas Publishing House pvt, ltd.1983.

In his *Die Nichtchristlichen Religionen,* Helmut von Glasenapp[14] points out that the *Rig Veda* is only a limited extent of the source of the subsequent directions in the various branches of Hinduism; *Rig Veda* is"... *noch im Kult verwendet, aber...[er] ist nicht mehr der eigentliche Quell religiöser Belehrung und Erbauung. Die meisten Hindus folgen in ihrem metaphysischen Vorstellungen und kultischen Riten vielmehr Werken der heiligen Überlieferung (smri), die von bestimmten als geschichtlich geltenden Heiligen wie Vyasa, Valmiki, Manu verfaßt sein sollen. Sie gelten als autorativ, weil sie behaupten, mit dem Veda übereinzustimmen, obwohl sie in Wirklichkeit vielfach von ihm abweichen...*" Or, as Max Weber[15] would have it "... *the Vedas contain nothing about the divine and human affairs fundamental to Hinduism. The three great gods of Hinduism, even their names, are hardly mentioned.*" and "*The Vedas rather defy the dharma of Hinduism. To a Christian, the official recognition of the Vedas might appear to be a 'formal principle' of Hinduism in the manner of the Protestant recognition of the Bible - always with the reservation that it is at least not absolutely indispensable.*"

A similar observation is offered in an earlier commentary on Indian religions by Edmund Hardy[16]: "*Der Veda . . . ist in den Augen der rechtgläubigen Inder, die ihr Urteil den (brahmanischen) Theologen unterordnen, eine Literatur von höchsten Ansehen in Glaubenssachen und hat*

---

[14] Von Glasenapp, Helmuth. Die Nichtchristlichen Religionen. Frankfurt: Fischer Bücherei. 1957. P.155.

[15] 1Weber, Max. *The Religion of India.* Glencoe, IL: The Free Press. 1958.

[16]Hardy, Edmund. *Indische Religionsgeschichte.* Leipzig: G. J. Göschen'sche Verlagshandlung. 1904

überhaupt eine nachhaltige Wirkung auf das Religionsleben Indiens ausgeübt, als dies bei andern heiligen Buch der Erde, vielleicht der Bibel ausgenommen, der Fall gewesen."

While it is not possible to know whether the supreme Indo-European god **dyāus*, the predecessor of Sanskrit *Dyāus*, was the godhead of a monotheistic religion, it does appear that the polytheistic pantheons of the individual Indo-European language families developed independent of each other and at a later time. It also seems clear that unlike the emergence of Christian saints out of earlier pagan gods, many of these gods represent the continuation of an even older indigenous religion. Be this as it may, the pantheon of gods of unequal rank, as we find it in the oldest forms of the Hindu religion, invites questioning into the relationship between these gods - questions as to which is superior, whether one of these might even be the source, the creator of all others, and ultimately, whether one or all might be eternal or whether their existence might transcend existence itself.

The Indo-European language groups all show a similar, apparent independent development of a hierarchy of deities that are the anthropomorphized spirits of the forces of nature. To some extent individual deities appear to have assumed features which were originally assigned to the unique 'sky' deity, e.g., the hurling of thunderbolts which the Roman Juppiter and Greek Zeus have brought with them from the IE deity and the Germanic deity *Thor* in his various Germanic garbs, who also hurls the thunder bolt. In Sanskrit *dyāus*, as in classical Greek and Latin versions, *Juppiter/Zeus* are also located somewhere in the heavens as are many, though certainly not all of the deities.

In Sanskrit the deities, it also seems to have their place in the heavens where Agni brings to them the food from the sacrificial offerings. Juppiter and Zeus also have associated with them the radiance characteristic of the sky deity and his close identification with the sun. But the great change comes in the ancient Sanskrit texts where this new and unique thought emerges, i.e., that the whole universe must have been created by one of those deities, or that it must have originated spontaneously, or it must have been eternally present. This is an idea that clearly did not come from the ancient Indo-European tradition; it is truly an innovation of the Hindu culture. Also inherent in this speculation is a notion of monotheism, i.e., the idea that only one of those many deities is the creator, i.e., that one of these *devas* is the creator of all the other gods. Alternatively it could be that the creator was yet another *force* not accounted for in the hierarchy of deities, or perhaps, it could be possible that even the notion that there are no other gods is also implicit in this idea.

The Hindu concepts of time and being are uniquely Hindu

The possibility that the universe was not created but was eternally present goes even further, suggesting, as it does, that there is no act of creative intent involved in the formation of the universe. These are ideas which have their origin uniquely in Hindu thought. They did not come from outside sources nor, as we have clearly seen, is there any indication that they were inherited from the Indo-European source culture or from any other source. This, then, is the answer to our original question "How much of Hindu thought was imported from the Indo-European source language?"

Several issues come into play in trying to compare the gods of these different cultures. First of all, it is an essential element of this examination that the gods themselves and the character of the pantheon of gods of each of these cultures are constantly in a state of change - as, indeed is everything that exists in this world. What we describe here must be of necessity being more like a running account of the history of the gods of the specific culture within a narrowly defined period of time. The gods venerated in India today and in particular those, which we have undertaken to describe here, have changed in the course of history from the time when we first encountered them. Our picture applies only to that earlier time and of limited validity, because we do not and cannot know the whole picture of the practices of that era.

A somewhat more remote element, yet of considerable significance for our consideration is the curious fact that the cultures introduced as examples here, all had an earlier cosmogony that viewed the world as having arisen out of chaos. In the Hindu tradition this has become an origin out of non-being, a vastly different concept. In the course of this inquiry several other uniquely Hindu creations not originally included in our question on the uniqueness of Hindu thought on time and being have emerged. One particularly significant Hindu development is the idea of the universe born out of non-being, which is one of the possible alternatives in the Vedic creation hymn. The possible Indo-European notion of a universe born out of chaos, i.e., out of a void, out of nothingness, became in the text of the Brhadāraṇyaka - one of the major books of the Upanishads, a universe described as originating out of nothingness, which is equated with death, and is also equated with hunger (see below for more on this notion).

The second, and still quite significant issue is the observation that the pantheon of gods of these several cultures is of relatively recent origin and specific to the particular culture, i.e., the various peoples did not bring the Indo-European godhead into their emerging culture, but instead, invented their own new gods. Even the very few elements imported from the earlier period have been drastically altered and are scarcely recognizable in their new homes. In other words, the gods of these cultures are unique to the specific cultures.

These speculations, in contrast with the apparent religious thought of the culture, where the arguments themselves occur in the context of discussions of the meanings of the ritual sacrifices, spread out into the neighboring civilizations and eventually became the basis for the monotheism of the religions of the world. It is the development of this concept and the accompanying notions about such concepts as *ātman-/prāṇa-*, time, and being which we will try to answer in the following pages. These are the questions introduced in the *Rig Veda* by a Hindu sage sometime around the end of the second millennium BC or the beginning of the first millennium BC. Clearly, the early Hindu speculations on the origins of being, time, and the nature of the vital force (*soul*) are exclusive to and of uniquely Hindu origin. The possibility that their ideas were borrowed from a neighboring culture or even influenced from foreign sources must be excluded because we can follow step for step the emergence of the Hindu concepts in the Hymns of the Rig Veda. Here is where we begin our search for the answer to the origin of these speculations.

PART II

THE ORIGIN OF THE WORLD IN HINDU THOUGHT

Language as the Source of Original Hindu Thought

In the long history of man's quest for answers to the basic questions of human existence, origin of the universe, origin of man, purpose of the universe, forces of nature (the motion of the stars, the whims of climate, etc.), man's role in life, and how one should live with others, the answers which are offered today to these questions do not come from recent discoveries in science and technology - as we are inclined to believe, but emerge instead directly from these ancient speculations. The mathematical calculations of Albert Einstein or Stephen Hawking and the philosophical ramblings of Martin Heidegger all derive from ancient speculations on these same basic questions. But, where do these speculations begin and where do our answers to these questions originate? In one of the hymns of the *Rig Veda* we encounter one of the earliest recorded explorations of the question of the origin of the universe. But this hard question ends here with an equally uncertain answer:

RV10: 129[1]

1. Nāsad āsīn nō sād āsīt tadānīm/
nāsīd rájo nó vyòmā parò yát/
kím āvarīvah kúha kásya šármann/
ámbhah kím āsīd gáhanam gabhīrám

non-*being existed* not, nor did *being exist* then, nor did space *exist* nor heaven beyond it. what *existed* moving? where what's shelter? what water *existed* deeply penetrated?

2. na mrtúr āsīd amŕtam ná tárhi/
ná rātryā áhna āsīt praketátah/
ānīd avātam svadháyā tád ékam/
tásmād dhānyán ná paráh kímcanāsa

death *existed* not, nor non-death there.
nor did the phenomenon of night-day *exist*.
it breathed without breath, autonomous, unique. nor did anything *exist*, yea, other than this.

3. táma asit támasā gūlham ágre/
'prketā salilā sárvam ā idám/
tuchyénābhv ápihitam yád āsīt/
tápasas tán mahinājāyataíkam
4. kāmas tád ágre sám avartādhī/
mánaso rétah prathamām

darkness *existed*, in darkness concealed in the beginning. an invisible flood all this.
whatever *existed* enclosed by void this alone
out of great heat (was) born.
lust overcame this in the beginning.
what first seed of thought *existed*,

---

[1]In the following text I have chosen to translate the Sanskrit forms of the root *as-* with English *exist*. Although this is awkward and still does not really convey accurately the Sanskrit meaning still it does serve to call attention to the difference in meaning of the Sanskrit word by giving it an English equivalent closer too the meaning in the text.

yád āsīt/
sátó bándhum ásati nír av-
indan/
hrdí pratīşya kaváyo manīşā

that discovered the bond of
being with non-being in
(the) heart of (the) *kavi*
wisdom.

5. tirašcīno vítato rašmír
eşām/
adháh svid āsīd upari svid
āsīt/
retodhā āsan mahimāna
āsan/
svadhā avastāt prāyatih
parástāt

their line stretched horizon-
tally.
whether something existed
below, whether above.
mighty beings *were* insemi-
nating, self-creations were
above inseminating down-
ward.

6. kó addhā veda ká ihá prá
vocat/
kúta ājātā kúta iyam
visrṣṭih/
arvāg devā asyá visár-
janenā-/
thā ko veda yáta ābabhūva

who knows certainly? who
here proclaims? whence
born? whence this creation?
the devas close by its crea-
tion-birth, and
then, who knows whence it
came-into-being?

7. iyám vísrşţir yáta
ābabhūva/
yádi vā dadhé yádi vā ná/
yo asyādhyakṣah paramé
vyòman/
só añgá veda yádi vā ná
véda

this creation whence it
came-into-being,
whether it was-made or not
made, if he did not make
this, whoever (the) wit-
nesses of this in the outer-
most heaven, he only knows
or he knows not.

* This translation uses italics where the verbs of being in the original have been translated.

There is one troubling, though seemingly trivial, which has occurred to me frequently in reviewing Sanskrit texts and their translations for this topic; this is the unintentionally misleading translation of Sanskrit into English. I have come to realize that the English words cannot easily be reconciled with the meanings of the original Sanskrit sources. Even such a frequent and apparently simple word as Sanskrit *devas* (and its plural form *devās*), usually translated as 'god(s)' or 'deity', invokes a Judeo-Christian image of the deities. Back in my student days in Germany our insightful Sanskrit teacher suggested on one occasion that he would prefer that we translate these words (Sanskrit *deva*, and the related lexical items) with the German word 'der Himmlische' which, alas, translates into English as 'the heavenly one.' At the time I assumed that he was invoking the historical origin of the root word with its meaning of 'sky, heaven', but I have come to understand the wisdom of his suggestion. He had most certainly reached the same conclusion as I now have and was trying to give a translation more commensurate with the Sanskrit meaning - a meaning that might even include the notions of 'sky, bright, heavenly, etc.' There are no words in English which could invoke the meanings of the Sanskrit words and, for this reason, I propose in the following texts to make a greater use of the original Sanskrit words - with appropriate introductory comments to caution readers of the problems which have prompted the choice.

In translating we encounter an even greater difficulty when we try to find a comparable meaning in English – or any other language, for that matter – for the Sanskrit words *ātma* and *prāṇā* both of which are often translated 'soul'. As I will explain at a later place in this essay both of these words originally (i.e., in the Rig Veda) had the meaning 'breath', but in the course of the development of the language they began to assume other meanings, one of which is that of the vital force, the life force which departs the body at death. But the word *ātma* goes even further, eventually taking on the additional meaning of the reflexive pronoun 'self.' Both continue to have the original meaning 'breath' in addition to the more recently acquired meanings. Translators have variously translated *ātma* as *self, soul* or *vital force.* The word *self* has found wide acceptance in translations, but ultimately it misleads the reader quite simply because it is used to denote not only that aspect of life which continues its existence after death, but it is also extended to include the Brahma, the universal 'being' from which all being emanates and is both the abode of all *being* and the *being* of all *being.* Aside from these more or less practical considerations there is also the grammatical aspect of this term which we should not take so lightly. *Ātma*, in the meaning of 'self' is after all, a pronoun and ought not be equated with the noun. This use also creates unnecessary conflicts in the original sources where *ātma* is equated with *prāṇā*, thus opening the door to additional inaccuracies in the translation of this second term. As was pointed out earlier, the English word *soul* is too closely bound to the Judeo-Christian concept of soul and too far from the meaning of *ātma* as it is used in our sources. I have elected to use the original terms as far as possible and where this did not seem appropriate, I have used the phrase *vital force* as the most suitable expression for the meaning of the particular texts.

In the Chāndogya Upanishad V, 1, 7[2] the five senses (*prāṇā*), i.e., speech, eye, ear, mind, and breath, turn to

[2]Translator Radhakrishnan, S. The Principal Upaniads; edited with introduction, text, translation, and notes by S. Radhakrishnan. London: George Allen & Unwin Ltd. 1953.

Prajāpati - their father - to settle the argument over which of them is the most important. He answers:

> "*He on whose departure from the body leaves it for the worst is the most important.*" Thereupon the *prāṇās*, each in succession, leave the body and on returning compare the damage. But when *prāṇā* (breath) is about to depart " . . . *tugging at the other senses like a spirited horse tugging at the stakes which hold it back*" the other senses surround him and ask him to remain, for he is the best of them. Whatever any one of them is, so they all are; i.e., if *prāṇā* prospers all prosper, etc. Thus all are called *prāṇā* because they all are *prāṇā*.

Here *prāṇā* is not only breath, but also all of the senses and also the vital force, which *is* life and when it departs, it takes life with it.

In contexts such as this, the translation 'breath' does not seem adequate, nor would the translation 'soul' be appropriate to the text. It seems prudent here to simply use the Sanskrit word, i.e., either *ātma* or *prāṇā*, or translate as 'vital force' and trust that the reader will make the reasonable adjustment for the broader meaning of the term.

While I am under no illusion that these lexical choices will or can actually convey the original Sanskrit meanings - and, in fact, I am certain that neither I nor anyone else truly knows precisely what those meanings were, I still hope that by making use of the original Sanskrit I will be able to help focus on the fact that we are treating a language and thought from a different time and a different culture. All translation, as everyone knows -- or should know -- is at the same time interpretation. When we look at the ancient Hindu (Vedic) texts we are examining elements of a culture that existed some three thousand years ago. We do not know what that culture was like and we do not what the original texts meant to those who created them or to those who heard them. We only have the unhappy certainty that our interpretation will err, but we can try to keep this error as small as possible and by working toward an understanding of these texts will be as objective as possible.

For the translations throughout this work I have tried to provide my own texts. However, I have relied heavily on Karl Friedrich Geldner's translations, since by virtue of his extensive knowledge of the literature and his caution in interpreting the texts seems to me, have had the more informed basis for his opinions. Similarly, Hermann Grassmann provides his *Wörterbuch zum Rigveda*[3] a well-founded expert opinion of the Vedic texts that I have made use of. Where I have used translations by other readers this is duly noted and credit is given to the translator.

The Key Text on Hindu Exploration of the Concepts of Time and Being

RV 10,129 provides the point of departure for most subsequent thought on the fundamental questions on the origins of the world and the involvement of the devas in the origins of all being. By examining the questions as they are posed in this text we should be in a position to enable ourselves to find the basis for the many arguments, the variety

[3]Grassmann, Hermann. *Wörterbuch zum Rig-Veda.* Wiesbaden: Otto Harassowitz. 1958.

of views, which follow.

This hymn begins with images of conditions in the absence of all signs of existence, the state before the emergence of the world. These images are followed by a series of interrogatives - e.g., *kim* 'what', *kusha* 'where', *kasya* 'whose', with more in the sixth stanza, e.g., *kas* 'who', *kuta 'whence', etc.* The hymn offers not just one answer, but a series of possible answers to the questions it poses, but these answers are in the form of possible solutions, but without any ultimate resolution of the question.

One particular difficulty in extracting these basic questions from the Vedic hymn lies in the suggested origins of the universe, which appears to have been widely misinterpreted. In the readings of stanza 5 the translations and interpretations have traditionally skirted or misunderstood the central imagery in this verse, e.g.:

> Stretched crosswise in their line, a ray of glory.
> Was there a below? And was there an above?
> There were sowers of seeds and forces of might:
> Potency from beneath and from on high the will.[4]

The original text has here:

> tiraščīno vítato rašmír eşām/
> adháh svid āsīd upari svid āsīt/
> retodhā āsan mahimāna āsan/
> svadhā avastāt práyatih parástāt

Note: *adhá*s 'there, in that (remote) place'; *svid* '*svid ... svid*: whether ... or'; *upari* 'upward'; *āsīt* 'it was'; *retodhās* '(those) inseminating (from *retas* 'seman' and *dhā*

[4]Translation by Jean Le Mée in: *Hymns from the Rig-Veda*. New York, NY: Alfred A. Knopf. 1975

'put, place)'; *āsan* 'they were'; *mahimānas* 'great, powerful beings'; *āsan* 'were'; *svadhā* '(its) own home ground'; *avastāt* 'below'; *parástāt* 'above'; *práyatis* 'presentation (of the *retas* = seman).') The translation into sowers of seeds does harm to the intended *insemination* and alters the meaning. 'Great beings inseminating, from above the presentation downward.' The image is an ancient, one common to many cultures: above the heavens, Sanskrit *dyāus*, masculine, and below the earth, Sanskrit *prthivī*, feminine, 'earth' in the act of procreation. The concept here appears to be rather of copulation between the *male* sky and the *female* earth which produces all life forms on earth. From above the semen - the liquid rain, which inseminates the earth below. In agrarian cultures where people live in close contact with the earth, this basic knowledge of how creatures reproduce is no mystery nor is the observation that after the rain new life appears in places where there was no visible life before. This is inherent in the belief in *spontaneous generation*, which was one of the early challenges to modern science. The author of this hymn, the *kavi*, has suggested, then, that something of this sort might be the source of all that exists, but this is just one possible answer to the question posed initially, and the *who*, *what*, *where*, *how*, etc., still remain to be answered.

Stanzas six and seven offer, in the form of questions, what is actually a series of possible origins of the universe. The questions: **Who** knows certainly? **Who** here proclaims? **Whence born**? **Whence this creation**? Were the *devas* close by at its creation-birth? And then, **Who knows whence it *came-into-being*? Whether it was-made or not made**, if there is a creator, then, **Whoever (the) witnesses of this in the outermost heaven, he only knows or**

or he knows not.

As posed here the questions (and the possible answers) are: the universe was born (spontaneous generation), or was it created (Was it made or not made? or is it forever there?). There could have been a witness (i.e., the question: was anything present before the *coming into being*? A creator beyond the world?). The *devas* may have been present before the beginning, they too may have been created, or have come into being spontaneously. In this list of questions one very important interrogative is missing; the question of *when* - and, curiously, contemporary thought on the origin of the universe points out that time is the essential element in being. Where time is absent being, is also absent.

From these possible answers follow the divergent views on the origin of the universe, which have been the object of much debate in subsequent generations and have provided the basis for the many divergent religious directions emerging from early Hinduism.

1. That the world is the result of an act of procreation - and this in turn brings the question of who or what is involved in this act, where it took place, etc.
2. That the universe is eternally present, uncreated and the world eternally perishes and is then recreated or born (uncreated) - with the *devas* appearing anew after each re-emergence and thus:
3. That the existence of the universe is itself cyclical or
4. That the world is created by an eternally and ever present creator or
5. That the world is not created but come into existence spontaneously (is born rather than created).

Within these possibilities the ***devas*** and even the creative force (which later becomes the **Brahma**, which then also becomes a *deva*) may be ever present or it may also be regenerated with each new coming-into-being with the Brahma being the sole eternally present creative force or, if the universe is eternal, **all** may be recreated with each new cycle within the eternal uncreated universe.

These many possible explanations later come to form the bases for the many directions which Hinduism and the religions growing out of Hinduism have taken. In the long course of development of the many variations of the original - which itself had no fixed body of religious dogma - the questions, or more correctly, the one great question that had occupied the minds of the Vedic thinkers seems to have gotten lost. Where the kavi of Vedas had sought to explain the origin of the world later thinkers provided answers to the basic questions without resolving the questions themselves. The host of different beliefs, which emerged, from this single source can be characterized with a few very general descriptions.

First, **monotheism**, is known to Western civilization through the Judeo-Christian religions, in Islam through a long history of various religious beliefs, recognizes generally only one, uniquc god as the source of all that exists and in its narrowest form, does not recognize any other attendant gods. This belief is not confined to the West or to Islam and is present in some form in many other world religions. The monotheistic god is a personal god as opposed to the impersonal god(s) of the pantheistic religions. God is viewed as the creator of the world who has set it in order. In this setting-in-order the monotheistic god is also the source of all natural laws with command over all the forces of nature. God is also the source of all laws governing ethical behavior, the one who punishes the bad and rewards good. A significant corollary of monotheistic beliefs requires that all appeals for exception to the laws of nature or of moral behavior must be directed to this one god; the god is unique and exclusive, as in the Bible (Ten Commandments) "*Thou shalt have no other gods before me.*" However, within the Christian tradition, we find the appeal to 'saints', i.e., to hallowed individuals whose assistance is invoked for intercession with god on the behalf of the petitioner. In some Christian communities these saints achieve the status of demi-gods and are worshiped almost as gods, though religious authorities do not recognize this practice. Often, these saints have their origin in older local deities who have been assimilated into the local Christian tradition and in this way perpetuate ancient beliefs. In similar ways, older religious traditions have certainly been assimilated into the Hindu beliefs and account in some measure for the expansion in the number of gods, not only in the Hindu religion, but also in the cultures of the related Indo-European language groups.

In Indian religious tradition the notion of a single source for the origin of the world led to the deification of Brahma, the creative force. This is one of the trio - the *trimurti* - of devas who head up the pantheon of Hindu devas. However, this god is the personification of the force that is introduced in the Upanishads as the personification of the absolute; he is not the supreme deva of the Brahmans (= Hindus), where the name refers rather to the religion, which has the Brahmans as priests. Brahma is generally regarded more as a demiurge with few followers and almost no temples dedicated to him. Hindus can be characterized as monotheists, but with many variations:

1. The theists who believe that god is separate from

and independent of the world and that all souls (ātman-/prāṇa-) and all that it contains are eternal though god is the ruler of all this.

2. Panentheists who believe that god is the effective and the material cause of the world, but with a part of his being beyond the world. This combines a pantheistic and theistic world-view.
3. The Vedanta Shankaras relegate Panentheism to a lower level of truth. Their ultimate truth is the Brahma, which stands above all duality of subject-object and all limitations of space, time, and causality.

The Upanishads have a variety of themes and emphases, generally toward a monistic and mystical philosophy. In some texts, the theistic element is more pronounced, as for example, in the Katha and the Shvetashvatara books of the Upanisads. The apparent contradiction between the theistic and the monistic views is not always perceived as mutually exclusive. One explanation is to be found in the Brhādaraṇyaka[5] III 9, 1[6]

---

[5]Cf. Swāmī Mādhavānanda (trsl.). The Brhadāraṇyaka Upaniṣad. Calcutta: Advaita Ashrama. 1965. Radhakrishnan, S. The Principal Upaniṣads; edited with introduction, text, translation, and notes by S. Radhakrishnan. London: George Allen & Unwin Ltd. 1953. Hume, Robert E. The Thirteen Principal Upanishads. Translated from the Sanskrit. 2nd. Rev. edition. London: Oxford University Press. 1968.

[6]*atha haināś vidagdhah śākalyah papraccha: kati devdāh, yājñavalkya, iti. sa haitayaiva nividā āpratipede, yāvanto vaiśvadevasya nividy ucyante; trayaś ca trī ca śatā, trayaś ca trī ca sahasreti. aum iti. Hovāca, katy eva devāh, yājñavalkya iti. trayaś trśad iti. Aum iti. hovāca, katy eva devāh, yāñavalkya, iti. a iti. aum iti. hovāca, katy eva devās, yājñavalkya, iti. traya iti. aum iti. hovāca, katy eva devās yājñavalkya, iti. dvāv iti. aum iti. hovāca,*

> 1. Then Vidagdha Shakalya asked him: 'How many devas are there, Yajnavalkya?' He answered, in accord with the following nivid (invocation of the devas). 'As many as are mentioned in the nivid of the hymn of praise to the Vishve-devas, namely, three hundred and three, and three thousand and three.' 'Yes," he said, 'but how many devas are there, Yajnavalkya?' 'Thirty three.' 'Yes,' he said, 'but how many devas are there, Yajnavalkya?' 'Six', he said. 'But how many devas are there, Yajnavalkya?' 'Two' he said. 'But how many devas are there, Yajnavalkya?' One and a half.' 'Yes', he said, 'but how many devas are there, Yajnavalkya?' 'One.' 'Yes', he said, 'but which are those three hundred and three and three thousand and three?

Yajnavalkya goes on to explain who these various devas are and in the end he declares that there is only one deva of whom all others come into existence:

> 9. They say this: If he blows as one, then how is he one and a half? So if in him he blows then all this comes about through him. 'Which is the one deva?' '*Prāṇa* (is the one deva). He is Brahman. Tyat he is called.'[7]

The contradictory views are a characteristic trait of the developing Hinduism where along with the fundamental āmonistic view a theistic view is gradually introduced. This is particularly noticeable in the doctrine and practice of bhakti, i.e., the acceptance of a personal deity who can be

---

katy eva devās, yājñavalkya, iti. adhyardha āum iti. hovāca, katy eva devāh, yājñavalkya, iti. eka iti. aum iti. hovāca katame te trayaš ca iti ca sahasreti.

[7]*tad āhuh, yad ayam eka ivaiva pavate, atha katham adhyardha iti. yad asminn idā sarvam adhyārdhnot, tenadhyārdha iti, katama eko deva iti. prāa iti, sa brahma, tyad ity ācakate*

invoked to intercede in human affairs. In the Bhagavadgita (probably 3rd or 4th century BC) a strikingly monotheistic view is to be found where the deva Krishna (an incarnation of Shiva) presents himself as an almost Christian-like, personal god[8]

59. yad ahākāram āritya na yotsya iti manyase mithyaia vyavasāyas te prakrtis tvā̃ niyokyati	59. If you think "having fixed on self-involvement so (I) has not fought." Then in vain you have thought this; nature will compel you to fight.
60. svabhāvajena kaunteya nibaddhah svena karmaṇā kartūṇecchasi yan mohāt kariṣyasy avašo 'pi tat	60. Through your own willfulness, Kunti son, bound by your own action, whatever through error you do not wish to do, you will even do that unwillingly.
61. išvarah sarvabhūtānā̃ hrddeše 'rjuna tiṣṭhati hati bhrāmayan sarvabhūtāni yantrārūḍhāni māyayā	61. The lord of all beings, Arjuna, resides in the heart, moving all beings by his magic on the great wheel of the universe.
62. tam eva šaranā̃ gaccha sarvabhāvena bhārata tatprasādāt parā̃ šānti	62. Into this refuge go, Bharat, with all your being. This, the highest tranquility,

[8]Cf. Bolle, Kees W. (trsl.). The Bhagavadgītā; New Translation. Berkeley: University of California Press. 1979. Sharma, Arwin. The Hindu Gītā. London: Gerald Duckworth & C. Ltd. 1986.Sinha, Phulgenda. The Gita As It Was. La Salle, Illinois: Open Court. 1987.

From serenity you will attain, (it is) firm, eternal.

63. iti te jñānam ākhyātā
guhyād guhyatarā mayā
vimršyaitad ašeṣeṇa
yathecchasi tathā kuru

63. So this knowledge is made known to you by me, the most secret from the secret. Consider this with diligence. As you want (to do), so do!

64. sarvaguhyatamā bhūyah
šrṇu me paramā vacah
ito 'si me drham iti
tato vakṣyāmi te hitam

64. This most all-secret word
hear this my ultimate speech:
You are my firmest sacraments, so I will tell you this, friend.

65. manmanā bhava madbhakto
madyāji m• namaskuru
mām evaiyasi satya te
pratijāne priyo 'si me

65. In (your) thought become devoted to me, performing rituals for me, bowing to me. Thus to me you will come, I promise, you are dear to me.

66. sarvadharmān parityajya
mām ekā šaraṇā vraja
ahta tvā sarvapāpebhyo
mokṣyiyāmi mā šucah

66. Having abandoned all laws
seek me alone as refuge.
I will free you from all evil.
Do not have regret.

This offers a monotheistic, personal god, but a loving, caring god.

In the polytheistic religious systems, gods - or more accurately, the anthropomorphized forces of nature, are seen as subject to laws. The forces may be arbitrary in their actions, but they are also governed by laws of their own and these laws can be used to control these same forces if onc understands how to manipulate the fundamental powers residing in the laws. Since the laws control the forces, i.e., the gods, and anyone who has control over these laws can control the forces, which are subject to them. The use of 'magic' formulas, rites, and rituals reflect the belief in the capacity of man to control the forces of nature. In a very real sense this belief in a sort of causality is essentially scientific, i.e., the recitation of the correct formula or the performance of the appropriate ritual necessarily effects the desired result and it follows that it is this action which has produced the result. Where the application of the strategy does not produce the desired effect, the failure can readily be attributed to the presence of even more powerful counter forces. In this we see the significant difference between religions based on belief in a diversity of gods and the monotheistic religions (such as Christianity and similar faiths): Christianity, by way of contrast, makes use of prayer in which the admittedly undeserving petitioner asks the supreme god to grant a boon which constitutes an act of grace for the petitioner. On the one hand we see in the polytheistic religions a universe governed by immutable laws which man can also exploit to his own benefit; while in a monotheistic world, we find a universe governed by immutable laws which the governing, creative force, and only this force, can, however, alter at its will.

In India polytheism is wide spread and a variety of cults worship all manner of gods from natural phenomena such as mountains (Kailasa, the Himalayas), rivers (Ganges, Yamuna), strangely shaped stones (Shiva's linga), plants such as the fig tree, or animals (apes, crocodiles, snakes, but especially cows). There are also the numerous local gods and the demi-gods who may be invoked to heal the sick, drive off evil and are the 'protectors of the world', the group of devas aligned with the points of the compass. These represent forces of nature and of social interaction: Kubera (north)- treasures of the earth, Yama (south) - realm of the dead, Varua (west) - water, Indra (east) - storms, Vayu (north-west) - the winds, Soma (north-east), Surya (south-west) - the sun, Agni (south-east) - fire. At the head of the pantheon stand the three chief devas in Indian religion, the *trimurti*: Brahma, Vishnu, and Shiva.

Where the question of the origin of the world arises, there follows the notion of the unique origin of all. But this immediately runs into existing polytheistic perceptions of the world, and some accommodation between the essentially conflicting views becomes necessary - at least for the more thoughtful questioner. This 'collision' of the two concepts can produce a monotheistic view, but more often it is a view which Max Mueller termed henotheistism and subsequent authors have called monolotry, i.e., the recognition of one god as the ultimate creative force, but without necessarily denying the existence of others as the monotheistic view does.

Yet another possibility presented in RV 10, 29 is that of a universe with no creative force - no god, an almost atheistic view, but still, atheism with a pantheon of devas.

The possibility of one, unique source for all the universe, of the first principle, is suggested in the creation hymn of the Rig Veda and later developed in the Upanisads, but the inherent incomprehensibility of this concept remains. The notion of 'nirvana', i.e., of the ultimate absorption of all into the one supreme reality, into the 'it' the '*tad ekam*' of the creation hymn "it alone breathed without breath, autonomous, unique" is a development which grows which grows out of just one of the various suggestions for the origins of the world found in the creation hymn itself. In subsequent speculations this 'it' finds many possible interpretations in the way in which it is related to the real world. The eternal, all-encompassing 'it' becomes, for example, the Brahma from which all that exists is derived and into which all being return.

Chandogya Upanishad VI, 10

1. imāh somya, nadyah purastāt prācyah syandante pašcāt pratīcyah tāh samudrāt samudram evāpiyanti, sa samudra eva *bhavati*, tā yathā tatra na viduh iyam aham *asmi* iyam aham *asmīti*.

   These rivers, my lad, flow from the east toward the east, the western to the west. They come from the sea and (go) into the sea. Thus this *is* (being in time) the sea. Thus, when there, these rivers do not know '*I am* (absolute being) this one,' '*I am* that one.'

2. evam eva khalu, somyemah sarvā prajāh satāgamya na viduh sata āgacchāmaha iti, ta iha vyāghro vāi siho vā vrko vā varāho vā kīo vā patago vā dašo vā mašako vā, yadyad *bhavanti* tad *ābhavanti*

   Even thus, my lad, all creatures having come from being do not know 'we have come from being.' These, then, tiger or lion or wolf or boar or worm or fly or horse fly or mosquito, whatever they *are* (being in time), that they *turn into*. (ā-bhavanti 'is coming into being')

3. sa ya eo 'nimaitadātmakam idam sarvam tat satyam sa ātmā tat tvam *asi* švetaketo iti. ...

> Just as this finest particle, all this, the true, the self (soul), this *is you* (absolute being), Shveketur.

Here is no personal god of Western religions nor god as creator of the universe, but the 'all' itself, omnipresent being out of which all being emerges and into which all being reverts, the Brahma. This does not posit a creative force or god, but instead assumes a continuous cycle of change in state of being, of coming into being and returning to the state of not-being. The distinction between absolute being and being as temporary - i.e., being in time, was clearly indicated in this text through the use of the two different verbs of being.

In studying the *Rig Veda* for what it can tell us about the development of the Hindu concepts of being and time we must not lose sight of the fact that the ideas which appear in RV 10, 129 are unique even in this large collection of hymns. The few other hymns, which seem to explore the origin of existence mention the problem only as a part of some broader topic. It is in *RV* 5, cited above that the question of the origin of being is one of several of the questions about the *deva* Agni. While this may be the sort of thought, which eventually leads to the larger question explored in RV 10, 129, it is only there that it becomes the central question. We should also bear in mind that the ideas expressed here and in subsequent works - notably in the Upanishads, specifically in the Bhadāraṇyaka, can not be said to represent the general trend in early Hindu thinking. While many of the Hindu seers have busied themselves with this impossible question, what we see expressed in these few works is but the thought of a minority. Thus it is that in the subsequent development of Hindu religion(s) we find the emergence of *devas* scarcely even mentioned in the

Vedic texts and these are the ones who become for most Hindus the primary representatives of their religion. The ideas first introduced in RV. 129 do not, however, disappear. As is clear, however, from the development, which follows, in the later works based on the Vedic literature they continue to occupy the minds of later seers, even if this is only a minority.

Note regarding the transition from the Vedic texts to the thinking of later seers on the origin of the world:

For man's interest in the origins of the world there are fundamental reasons which lie outside the area of philosophy or theology. From Immanuel Kant's epistemology and the subsequent substantiation of his conclusions through psychological and neurological evidence; it has become more comprehensible to us that our human perception of causality and of time is a consequence of the basic way in which the human brain interprets the sensations it receives from the real world. The conviction that there must be an explanation for all existence is thus the consequence in part of the limits of man's inherent ability to perceive reality. Kant reasoned that the human mind adds the elements or categories of time and space to its sense perceptions in its contact with the surrounding world. The notion of causality arises out of this process of the mind and makes the notion of prior cause for all events a necessary part of the perception of reality. Recent discoveries in the field of neurology and psychology have been able to confirm the truth of Kant's observations on the basis of recorded cases of patients who have lost this ability of the human brain to add the element of time to their perception of reality and have thus lost contact with the past and with the sense of causal relationship[9]. Because of this perception of causality it seems thus obvious to us that there must be some primordial cause for all that exists, i.e., some sequence of events which would ultimately explain all subsequent reality, some Thomistic 'first cause'. The questions, which the author of RV 10, 129 posed and ultimately found unanswerable, have certainly challenged later thinkers, but the impossibility of answering this question has not prevented man from attempting to offer solutions where there can be none.

Also of critical importance for our considerations are the Kantian categories, which enter into the picture, when we begin to examine the beginnings of the Hindu concepts of being, time, and soul (better: *ātman-/prāṇa-*). We have seen that the concepts of time and being which emerge in early Hindu thought are not the continuation of an inherited concept, but rather an original Hindu creation. But if this idea is not inherited, then where did it originate? There is another source for much of our innovative ideas and this is language itself. I do not mean here the sort of etymological speculation, which will be discussed farther along in this text, but rather in the language itself, in its grammar and structure. These ideas could have come from any other language, however, had other thinkers been as astute as the ancient Hindus. The language, however, owes its recognition of time and being to the basic processes of the human mind which adds these elements to all sensory perception. This is ultimately the source of Hindu thought on time and being and this is where the Kantian categories can

---

[9] Among other sources one can consult: Oliver Sacks. *The Man Who Mistook His Wife for a Hat*. New York: Harpur and Row. 1987.

help us to understand the implicit assumptions of their reasoning.

The ancient Indian culture had an early interest in the phenomenon of language and explored it in far greater depth than any other culture has ever done. This grew out of the oral tradition of the Vedic and Sanskrit literature. The hymns are transmitted from individual to individual and generation to generation in an oral tradition. This involves an elaborate system for memorization through repeated syllable by syllable recitations in several different configurations of the lines of the hymns. Down to the present the tradition continues, but the reciters had begun to notice in the early centuries of the tradition that some of the language of their most sacred texts was becoming incomprehensible as their own spoken language changed. To avoid what clearly seemed to be the imminent loss of the meanings of the texts they began assembling collections of explanations of more obscure words and phrases. By the time of the grammarian Pāini these early 'linguists' had developed along with these collections a system for the description of the language which he was able to codify into a grammar more thorough than those of the European grammarians of later times. Thus in ancient India the works of later grammarians such as Kautsa, Yāska, whose works are lost to us as a consequence of the great authority which Pāṇini (circa 400 BC) had achieved, there continued a tradition which had begun with the *Nighaus*, the name given to the major collection of glossaries (in 3 sections) along with the later commentaries of Yāska and the *niruktas*, i.e., etymologies or explanations of obscure text occurrences. These collections, which had begun quite early in the Vedic tradition, reflect both the profound interest which the Hindus had in this literature as, too, their continued preoccupation with language itself. This exploration of the phenomenon of language was an active pursuit of the contemporaries of the authors of the Upanishads, perhaps even of some of these authors themselves.

Down to the present time the works of the Hindu grammarians have shown us more insight into the phenomenon of language than even most of the recent developments in our own culture. This interest in grammar is not, however, to be separated from a more active interest in the phenomenon of language itself and thus it is more likely that the Hindu thinkers occupied with language also reflect this broader phenomenon.

Within the sacred texts this interest in the phenomenon of language itself becomes involved on several different levels. In some instances it is word analysis - deriving the word root and associating the many meanings which one particular root or seemingly related words may collectively convey.

The Vedas were followed by the Brāhmaṇas which provided information on or theological explanations in prose of the rituals connected with the Vedic texts. In connection with the Brāhmaṇas are subsequently the Āraṇyakas which begin the theological / philosophical speculations on the Brāhmaṇas, which the Upaniads continue, but in even greater depth so that these become far removed from the basic ritual character of the Vedic texts.

Of the numerous Upanishads the Bhadārayaka is the one in which the ideas in RV 10, 129 receive the most extensive consideration and here we find voice given to the differences in the arguments anticipated in the Vedic hymn. Bhadāraṇyaka: Second Brāhmaṇa: 1;

naiveha kĩ ca nāgrā āsīd / mrtur-naivedam āvrtam āsīt - ašnāyayā / ašnāyayā hi mrtuh / tan mano 'kūruta; ātmanvī syām iti | so rcannacarat / tasyārcata āpo jāyantda arcate vai me kam abhūd iti / tad evārkasyārkatvam / ka ha vā asmai bhavati ya evam etad arkasya arkatva veda |	There was nothing here in the beginning. This was covered by death - by hunger, hunger is death. It brought forth the mind (thinking): "let me be ātman*. Worshiping he went about [and] from this water was generated: "while I was worshiping what came into being" This 'arka'-ness, that 'arka' comes to him, who knows thusly the 'arka'-ness of 'arka'.

* ātman = myself, but here it is also a play on *manas* 'mind' in the previous line.

The last lines of this passage from the Bhadārṇayaka are usually translated: "*He moved about worshiping. From him worshiping (arcan, present participle, nominative singular, masculine of arc- 'worship, shine, etc.') thus, water was produced. Lo: 'As I was worshiping (carate, locative singular, masculine, absolutive, of the present participle of arc-), water appeared'; Therefore, water (arka) is called fire (arka). Water surely comes to one who knows thus the reason why water (arka) is called fire (arka).*"

In this passage one sees a significant example of the multifaceted role which language analysis plays in the Hindu religious speculations; here the Sanskrit word 'arka' which can have a number of different meanings is taken back to its original form, i.e., an etymology, which was the

Sanskrit root *arc-* meaning 'to shine, to be brilliant' whence it takes on meanings having to do with *brightness*. This meaning can expand to include *to praise* or *worship*, i.e., to exhibit that *brightness* which emanates from the practicing ascetic and proceeding from this meaning the root can take on the meaning *to sing*. The noun assumes further meanings including ' heat, hymn of praise, one who praises; sun; the male member' and eventually even 'fire' as it appears in the very next chapter of the cited text. In the present passage the meaning 'brightly shining' is extended to the shining drops of perspiration, i.e., of water, while *brightness* and *heat* can mean also *fire* -, i.e., 'the brightly shining'. Hence the 'fireness of water'. The author of this passage, through an intricate reasoning process and with the use of the vocabulary of this text, has cleverly deduced from the words which he uses the true origin of all that exists, i.e., from desire, heat, then from heat comes water and also fire. This rather complex reasoning reminds one of the writings of the medieval German mystics *Heinrich Suso*, *Meister Eckehart*, and *Mechthild von Magdeburg* or of the 18th century German *pietists* and the 19th century *natural philosophy*, an outgrowth of German Romanticism, or, from this century, of the writings of *Martin Heidegger* and other contemporary followers of the medieval and 19th century mystics.

The word for hunger in this passage is derived from the Sanskrit root *aś-* 'to eat', or, more precisely, from its desiderative form *aśanāyā* 'desiring to eat'. Here we find an even more subtle use of language. *Death* is a form of *asat* 'non-being' - which has the potentiality of being. The equation with 'hunger', i.e., hunger as the desire to eat, thus implies in non-being the element of desire, in this case the desire for being, the essential desire for life. Thus 'covered by death, by hunger. Hunger is death' gives the sense of *asat* with the implicit potential as well as the desire for *sat*. The inclusion of desire in this choice of words places in turn an implicit intent on the act, which brings about the emergence of being out of nothingness. This, then, is one answer to the questions raised in the creation hymn of the Rig Veda: being is created out of non-being through a conscious act of will.

The following paragraph from the same Second Brāhmana;

2 *Water, lo, is arka. That which was the froth of the water became solidified; that became the earth. On it he rested. From him thus rested and heated (from the practice of austerity) his essence of brightness came forth (as) fire.*[10]

This passage continues the image purveyed in the first passage and explains in more detail the identity of fire and water. From this water comes that element, the foam, which solidifies to become the solid earth. From the heat of the creating being, that heat which results from contemplation, came fire, and once again we have the play on the root *arc- /ark-*.

In this oral tradition of poetry the language-conscious Hindu poets, the *kavi*, present their own thoughts on the profound religious questions and in this language they seek the answers to the questions they have posed. Speech itself, i.e., language (Sanskrit *vāc-*) is sacred. It is

[10]Translations consulted also include: *The Principle Upaiads.* S. Rachakrishnan, editor and translator. London: George Allen & Unwin Ltd. 1968; *The Bhadāraṇyaka Upaniad.* Swāmī Mādhavānanda, transl. Calcutta: General Printers & Publishers Limited. 1965.

carried from the speaker's mouth on the *prāṇā*, the vital force of the individual, the part of the whole of the universe. Thus speech/language with its connection to the life force of the universe is also the residence of knowledge of the origin of the universe and of all that is in it. For the *kavi* it remains only to retrieve the knowledge which lies intertwined with all other elements of speech and bring this knowledge to light in order to unravel the mysteries of the universe. This particular use of language is a later development in the religious tradition and not to be found in the Vedic texts where the role of language is more subtle. In the Vedic hymns in the treatment of the origins of being language itself supplies underlying concepts of time and change in time, but without a conscious awareness of this distinction on the part of the kavi.

Aspects of Verbs of Being in Sanskrit

We may be inclined to assume that the Hindu thinkers in the early part of the first millennium before the beginning of our time reckoning had already begun to investigate the concept of time pretty much as the natural consequence of their contemplations on the questions of the origins of all that exists. But speculations on the nature of time require a prior recognition of time as a specific concept and Hindu thought had not yet reached this recognition. Thus Sanskrit has the familiar expressions for adverbs of time as a relative concept, e.g., *adya* 'today', *švas* 'tomorrow', *hyas* 'yesterday', *adhunā* 'now', *tadā* 'then', etc., or as a measure, e.g., *ahan* 'day', *māsa* 'month', or terms for a fixed time as in setting the time for some specific event, e.g., *kāla* masc. "specific point in time". But expressions for time as an abstract concept are absent. Thus, for example, such questions as whether the creator of the universe is a part of his creation or separate from it and whether the creator stands within time - as a part of his universe - or stands outside of time, are not within the realm of the early Hindu thought. In these earliest speculations time is regarded (again, implicitly only) as an essential aspect of the concept of being; it is not taken to be a separate and distinct element and is therefore not isolated or abstracted from the concept *being*. However, when we set out to examine the concept of time as it is used in Hindu thought of this early period we find that the grammatical and semantic aspects of the language used in the speculations of the Hindu thinkers readily yield insight into the underlying, implicitly included element of time and we are obliged to take these aspects of language under consideration.

Adverbs of time, e.g., *now*, *then*, *when*, *today*, *tomorrow, yesterday*, or the nouns such as *day*, *night*, *month*, etc., and the more subjective aspects of time implicit in the verb tenses, e.g., the aorist with its implicit notion of action completed in time, or the perfect tense which includes the meaning of action begun at a past time with its consequences carrying over into the present, all implicitly convey the meaning of time. But the concept of time itself as an abstract notion is not one that has been isolated from other meanings. The grammatical expressions of time do implicitly represent aspects of concepts of time, aspects that are not present in the specific adverbs and nouns, which define the more tangible attributes of time.

All languages do, of course, have nouns for aspects of time, but in early Sanskrit these words concern time as a measuring stick or time as a quantity, not the abstract concept of time. The words for *day*, night, and *month* as quantities have already been mentioned, but one designation for time, the word *kāla,* in particular attained special significance in the early religion and this word subsequently underwent a special development in the emerging religions of India. This Sanskrit word for time, *kāla* masc. "specific point in time", is of a similar origin as the Sanskrit (Vedic) word *kalā* fem. "a small part of the whole, one sixteenth, a bit", both derived from the root *kal-* "calculate, count." *Kāla* gives what is essentially a quantitative definition of time which, as Hindu thought later develops, is extended from this essentially limiting definition to the new meanings which still follow much within the boundaries set by the original meaning of the word. That is to say that the semantic field in the expanded meaning still very much keeps to a quantitative definition of time. Some very insightful dissertations on the subject of time from this particular vantage point have appeared in recent years. Sundar Raj[11] has presented a thorough scholarly study of the origins of concepts of time and measurement of time in which he has focused particularly on Vedic texts. Here Raj examines such aspects of time as the establishment of the seasons and regular recurrences of astral phenomena. In another, far broader and also thorough study of the ancient concepts of time in India and the influence of these concepts on other cultures Dr. Vedavyas[12] has looked into the divisions of time such as those we have just reviewed and extended this study to the area of astrology and the spread of this phenomenon into other cultures.

The noun *kāla-* occurs only once in the Rig Veda:

---

[11]Raj, Sundar M. Time. Rg Vedic Studies. Series III. Madras: International Society for the Investigation of Ancient Civilization. 1983.

[12]Vedavyas, Dr. Science of Time. Hyderabad: University of Sciences. 1997.

10,42,9 *utá prahám atidīvyā jayāti kṛtám yác chvaghnī vicinóti kālé* "and in the game having cast (the die) he wins, whatever the player wins accumulates in (that) time." But later Sanskrit literature allows the meanings associated with this word to expand its semantic field to cover a broad range of meanings, especially in the general area of meaning of time as a limit: e.g., a fixed time, period of time or time in general, but also extending to: season, proper time, etc. Cf. *kālah prasthānasya* "time for departure"; *kālo yad bhuñjīta bhavān* "It is time for you to eat", or *šaṣthe kāle* "in the evening of the sixth day', or Prāt. *kāla* "metrical measure", *kālasya dīrgasya* "after some time", *kālakaraṅa* neutr. "fixing a time", *kālakṛta* "appointed for a certain time."

Deriving from this semantic nucleus of a 'time within which' comes a far more significant extension of the meaning of fixed or limited time to the sense of the final time or limit of life, i.e., 'death', e.g.: *kāla-* "death by age, destiny, fate", and from this new semantic nucleus come compound words containing this basic meaning of death, e.g.: *kālam kṛ-* "to die"; *kālagata* "dead, lit. 'time-gone'." Associated with this semantic field are further extensions of the meaning of death in a number of other compound words. Thus we find, for example: *kālacodita* "summoned by death", *kāladaa* (with *daṇḍu-* "staff") "the staff of death", *kāladūta* (with *dūta-* "messenger") "angel of death", *kālatulya* "like death, deadly", *kāladamanī* "death-conqueror, cognomen of Durgā", *kāladharma-* "the law or operation of time, death", *kālavikrama* masc. "the power of time, death", *kālarātrī* "the night of all-destroying time, night of the destruction at the end of the world - often personified as Durgā or one of her Šakti; also: the night of a man's death; a particular night in the life of a man - the seventh day of the seventh month of the seventy-seventh year, after which he is no longer obliged to adhere to the customary ordinances."

As a development from this semantic innovation, i.e., the association of time with death, the word *kāla* begins to occur with increasing frequency in contexts in which the name of Yama, the *god* of the underworld, is found. From this originate compounds such as: *kālapāśa-* "Yama's noose = death", *kālarūpadhṛṣ* "wearing the form of Yama or death."

The association of time with astronomy, the movement of the stars, periodic change, and with astrology also leads into new semantic fields. 1) with the movement of the stars: *kālajña* "knowing the fixed times or seasons", *kālatā* "seasonableness, timeliness", *kālaparyaya* masc. "the revolution or course of time." From these designations for seasons and times follow then the references to the stars by which the seasons and fixed times are measured: *kālayukta* masc./neut. "the fifty-second year in the sixty year cycle of Jupiter", *kālakrt* masc. "producing time, seasons; the sun", or the name of the astronomical work *kālasamhitā*. In an impressive study of the Hindu concepts of time Vedavyas[13] examined European reports on the achievements of Hindu astronomy and on the spread of the astrological findings of these early scientists. The recognition from European scholars of the enormous knowledge, which Hindu scientists had amassed in their scientific probing, has not been lacking. But Vedavya's most significant contribution lies in his own investigation the astronomical bases for the divisions of time and on the Vedic origin of astrology which

[13]Vedavyas. *Science of Time*. Jubilee Hills, Hyderabad: University of Vedic Sciences. 1997.

also merit our consideration in the following pages.

The many different concepts emanating gradually from the central meaning of the original word for time finally came united and coalesced into grander concepts of the nature of the universe and of existence. Time as a finite quantity measures the lives of men and gods; it has beginning and end while time as it is measured in the motions of the heavenly bodies becomes the measure of time itself. Time as measured in the recurring events in the universe, i.e., in the seasons and astronomical events is inherently circular in nature and gives rise to a concept of time - the abstract notion - as essentially circular, but with one great anomaly: somewhere within this concept time has beginning and end. But where does this concept of time lead in Hindu thought?

The concept of the cosmos as it emerges from these concepts of time is essentially cyclical; it is a cosmos passing through endless cycles of birth and death, of the beginnings and the ends of the endless cycles. There is transmigration of the soul (i.e., the *ātman-/prāṇa-*) of every being with reward for good deeds through the elevation in the hierarchy of life in the next life and punishment for evil in the subsequent incarnations. Even the devas are included in the cycles with the ultimate exception of one idea, that of the eternal Brahma - which is neither a god or a deva, and recognized in virtually all branches of Hinduism, Buddhism and other religions which have grown out of Hinduism. In keeping with the sense of the word for time there are the *kālpa*, the cycles of the universe, each with its beginning or dawn and end or twilight (note: *kālasūrya* masc. "the sun at the end of the world") is measured in specific quantity. The measurements of time in this astronomical concept are:

> The Brahma-day = *kalpa* which ends in a partial end of the world. The kalpa = 1,000 great world ages = maha-yuga. One mahayuga = 320,000 human years
> each mahayuga consists of four yugas:
> Krita, Treta, Dvampara, and Kali occurring in diminishing series from 4, 3, 2, and 1 thousand 'god-years' each of which corresponds to 320 human years. Each yuga has a dawn and a twilight, which takes up an additional one tenth of the yuga.

The dimensions here are, of course, enormous, measuring the vast universe - and the lives of men - ultimately against the rotations of the pole star.

The development of the concept of time in the Hindu tradition evolves out of the original semantic nucleus of the designation for time (*kāla*) and stays generally within the semantic boundaries set by the original meaning. But the philosophical definition of the meaning of time as it is contained in the Sanskrit verbs of being does not occur because the concept of being itself implicitly includes time as an essential aspect of being in time as opposed to being outside of time. The inclusion of time in the concept of being thus hinders and prevents the isolation or abstraction of an absolute concept of time independent of being and separate from time as a quantity. Nor is this concept of time as an aspect of being in any way compatible with the concepts of time contained anywhere in the meanings which are added to the word *kāla*. The latter continues its independent development with the same word is still present in Hindi today.

M. Sundar Raj[14] in his examination of the origins of

---

[14] M. Sundar Raj. Ibid.

concepts of time in the Rig Veda cites texts in which "father time" Tvastr is named. Sundar Raj is especially aware of the difficulty which man experiences in formulating concepts about time: "Man's awareness of Time is purely experiential; he cannot formulate concepts about it. The discussions about Space-Time of modern physics falls into the same category. It does not explain what these things mean. It only says how they work in man's experience of life. The difference is that it employs highly technical mathematical language much beyond the understanding of most persons including scientists themselves." But here again the author has emphasized the origins of divisions of time - seasons, etc. - rather than the fundamental abstract concept which occupies modern scientific discussion.

There is, however, another source for the definition of time and the distinctions, which can be made in the concepts of time. This source is the language of the thinkers itself. The older language and, thus too, the older speculations about being made significant differentiations based on time in their arguments, but these time distinctions are not consciously made; they are implicit in the language used. This is a difficult concept, but it is essential in understanding the arguments, which I will present in the next few pages. An illustration from our own language will aid in making the basic concept more readily accessible to the reader.

Every language has a vast inventory of grammatical meanings which its users use and understand, of which they are, however, not consciously aware. For example, the English verb *sing*, as in the sentence *She sings* can mean that *she* presently engages in this activity or has the capacity to sing - as an absolute without the inclusion of its apparent present tense aspect. This contrasts with *She is singing* which has a durative meaning and can be taken to mean that *she* is presently engaged in this particular on-going activity. In each of these grammatical variations there is an aspect of time and in one case even the absence of time (i.e., *she sings* as an absolute), but with each of these cases there is a specific, unique meaning which the speaker of the language intends.

There are other aspects of time whose meaning is inherent in verbs themselves. The inchoative verb, for example, contains the notion of an action, which has a starting point in time with its anticipated end at a later time included in the meaning of the verb. That is to say that the action occurs or is occurring over a period of time beginning with one state or condition and continuing to the new state. As an illustration, the verb *thaw* denotes an action beginning in one state - that of the unthawed substance - and continuing to the new state - the thawed substance. In English, however, this verb is in reality two different verbs, one is the intransitive as in *The ice on the river is thawing.* But the second verb is transitive as in *Rebecca is thawing the ice.* Both verbs include in their meaning two different states and the notion of change - in time, of course, in the intransitive, inchoative verb the notion is of the thing itself undergoing the change of state; in the transitive some external force causes this change and this is included in the verb. Using these verbs in speech the speaker knows intuitively the different meanings. But this is not conscious knowledge; the speaker is not conscious of these grammatical distinctions. And in the history of the study of language we see that it has taken grammarians centuries - even millennia - to recognize and name these seemingly obvious distinctions.

In this example of the inchoative verb the speaker knows the meaning of the words he uses and does not have cause to further clarify this in using it in a real situation. The knowledge is, of course, based on experience, i.e., we know of the change of state from an initial state to a final state and this knowledge is present in language; we can express it in language. It also follows from this that language is a veritable treasury of knowledge about the real world extracted from experience even though the speakers of the language are rarely conscious of this knowledge. Language itself can thus become a source of information about the world, i.e., it may be possible to bring this knowledge to a conscious level of awareness just as grammarians have done in making distinctions among the many different grammatical meanings. In the key Vedic text (RV 129, 10) on the origin of being the kavi has made use of the difference in meaning between two Vedic verbs of being in his speculations on the role of time in the origin of the world.

There is a general belief that every concept, which the human mind can invent, can also be treated in language. Our belief is, of course, erroneous. When Socrates demonstrated that humans have innate understanding of the principles of the Pythagorean theorem he made use of pictures drawn in the sand to convey meanings, which are not achievable through language[15]. But there are things, which the mind can suspect but can neither truly comprehend or name. Such products of the human imagination defy the capacity of language to convey meaning or to act as a tool in the thought process. Such are the speculations on the origin of the universe, on the origin of man. Hindu thinkers in earlier times, like the medieval German mystic Meister Eckhart or the philosopher Thomas of Aquinas or Jacob Boehme, or, in this century, Martin Heidegger, took on the

[15] Plato, Dialogues. Meno, 82, b ff.

task of speculating on the nature of being and time which necessarily compelled them to struggle with the limitations of language in describing the indescribable. In the following pages I have attempted to find the more precise meaning of the words for *being* used in the Rig Veda in the speculation on the origin of being by examining the origin of the words and tracing their historical development. This is followed by a very brief discussion of the use of the words in the specific text.

In Sanskrit, specifically in one particular hymn of the Rig Veda, speculation on the origin of being led to the attempt to capture the incomprehensible and inconceivable in words, without at the same time losing the key elements in the speculation in the struggle with the inadequacies of language. The kavi - or philosopher-poet - who composed these few verses of Rig Veda 10,129 made use of distinctions between the Sanskrit verb root *as-* "be, exist", i.e., being without the element of time, and *bhū* "be, become", i.e., exist in time. The following discussion considers the origin and meaning of these two verbs and their application in speculation on the nature of being.

There are, however, two fundamental difficulties in the discussion of the verbs of being in Sanskrit, which have bearing on this presentation:

> 1. Sanskrit inherits two verbs of being from the parent language, i.e., Indo-European. Although there is some unavoidable overlap in the mind of the speaker on the meanings of these two verbs there is a fundamental differentiation in the meanings which separates the second verb of being from the original Indo-European verb **es-*, Sanskrit *as-*. This second verb, Sanskrit root *bhū-*; *bhavati*, "he is" undergoes a transition in Sanskrit and takes

on the meaning "become". A similar change in this particular verb root is to be found in almost all the related Indo-European languages. The question then becomes: What is the basis of this original distinction?
2. A part of the difficulty in describing what semantic distinctions were created between these two verbs of being in Sanskrit lies in the language in which we are attempting to describe the phenomenon, i.e., in this case the problem in description lies in part in limitations in the English language. The original basis for the differentiation in meaning lies in the recognition of the distinctions in the fundamental concept of being, but there is no similar distinction in English and the sensitivity to the necessity for this distinction is not readily found here. Thus the necessary vocabulary is missing in English and even the sense of this difference in meaning is differently perceived thus making the description of the Sanskrit development arduous.

The meanings of the two Sanskrit verbs are based on modifications of semantic aspects of two verb roots inherited from the parent Indo-European language. The basic meanings of the two roots can be derived, however, through comparison with related languages where the meanings are still present and their subsequent development - i.e., the creation of new words from the original verb roots - expands on the picture of the semantic area included in the inherited root.

We can begin with Indo-European **es*- "be"; the copula and substantive verb. This root was originally limited in its meaning to the sense of *exist*, i.e., the substantive meaning without the inclusion of time. In Sanskrit as in many other Indo-European languages, the verb was not used as the copula or was only rarely used. Derivatives from this verb root in the various Indo-European languages include: Sanskrit (present participle) *san* (m.), *sat* (n.), *satī* (f.) with the meaning 'being' but also: 'good, true' = Avestan *hant-*, *hat-*; Sanskrit *satyam* "truth"; Lat. *sons* (*sontis*, genitive) "guilty"; Greek τὰ ὄντα "present, truth; obsession"; Germanic **sanþa-* "true", Old English *sóð* "true." Old Norse *sannr* 'true' (from Germanic *sanda), Gothic **sunjis* 'true' (from Germanic *).

The second verb root with the meaning of *be* is Indo-European: **bheu-/*bhū-* with the probable original meaning of *grow, flourish*; The basic present tense meaning of Indo-European **es-* as the substantive verb, leads in several Indo-European languages to the use of Indo-European **bheu-*, etc. as a suppletive in the conjugations of the verb for *be*. In Latin the forms of Indo-European **bheu-* constitute the basis of the perfect tense: Latin *fuī* "I have been", from the Indo-European **bheu-*, stands along side the present tense *est* 'is', while in Greek this root is represented in the present tense form φὺω "I father, generate", φὺομαι 'I grow, become', and the preterit ἔφυν "I became", πεφύκα perfect tense 'I am', with the abstract noun φῦσις 'nature'. In the Germanic languages the proximity in meaning with Indo-European **es-* lead to a contamination in the actual forms of the verbs of being, producing variant forms with initial *b-* in combination with the original forms of the Indo-European verb root *es-*; thus Old English has two forms *béo* "I am" from Indo-European **bheu-*, and *eam*, *eom*, *am* "(I) am" (Germanic (Gothic) *im*, and Old Norse *em*); contamination of the two verb forms yields Old English OE. *béom* 'I am', which corresponds to Old High German *bim* 'I am'. The meaning "dwelling" for the Indo-European root **bheu-* also shows up frequently in Indo-

European languages: Cf. Old Norse *buð* "dwelling", Lithuanian *būkla* "dwelling", and more.

Sanskrit *bhū-* has the meanings: become, come into being; occur, happen; become something; be (with nominative) - not 'being' but as dependent on circumstances, temporary; to persist; become apparent; be concealed, become concealed; be effective, helpful; desire to be.

Sanskrit uses *as-* as the copula or in the meanings:

1. Exist, be alive, active
2. Be present (at), be in a state, belong to (with the dative case), etc.

In English *be* is most generally used as a copula or in the meanings: to be present (at), be in a state, etc. The past tense of this verb of being in English is formed from an Indo-European root **wes-* "tarry, remain." In English the meaning of being in time is conveyed with the verb *become* which is used to indicate change in being while being without time is given with the verb *exist* to indicate the fact of being, being without the semantic element of duration.

In English:
be is most often used as the copula;
become is used to indicate change in being
exist to indicate the fact of being, being without duration or time

Sanskrit uses *as-* as:

1. Copula; example: tat tvam *asi* švetaketo 'that, Shvetaketur, *is* you'
2. Exist, be alive, active; example: *asīd* rājā nalo nāma 'there was a king named Nala'
3. Be present (at), be in a state, belong to (w. dative), etc.; example: pra yah senānir adha nrbhyo *astī*nah satvā gaveṣaṇan sa drṣṇuh (astīnah = asti + inah)

English be:

1. Copula;
2. Be present (at), be in a state, etc.
3. The past tense of this verb of being in English is formed from an i.e., root **wes-* "tarry, remain."

The range of meaning of these verbs in Sanskrit as reflected in words formed from these verb roots in Sanskrit:
Sanskrit past participle *bhutáh* "become"; *bhūtám* "creature"; *bhavítram* "world"; *bhū* "earth", *bhútih* "well being, good state (of health), growth, etc." and many more. "dwelling", etc.

In the development of these two verbs (Sanskrit *bhavati* and *asti*) outside Sanskrit we are able to see the direction the basic meanings from IE have taken. The use of the IE. root **bheu-* in the West Germanic languages and in the Baltic languages shows an extension of the root meaning of being and change in time, of "tarry" in the nouns meaning *dwelling*, etc. The use of this same root in Latin in the formation of the perfect tense of the verb which has the Latin present tense form *est* 'is', shows that the essentially different meaning of the two verbs of being is particularly significant. Those words derived in Sanskrit from the two verb roots (Indo-European **es-* and **bheu-*) give some indication of the aspects of their basic meanings which are unique to Sanskrit. For example: *sánt-* m., *sát-* n., and satī f. 'being (present participle), true, good' *sva-stí-* m. 'Subordinate, servant', *abhi-sti* f. 'Help, aid'.

For the copula, however, Sanskrit most frequently does without the aid of any verb form. In the famous 'Indra" hymn (RV 2, 12), for example, the repeated Indra phrase never uses the copula:

yō jāta eva prathamō ma- nasvān	Who (was) first-born, the wise one,
devō devān kratunā pary- abhūṣat	deva served the devas with strength,
yasya šuṣmād rodasī ab- hyasetā̃	whose rush both worlds feared,
nrmṇasya mahnā, sa janāsa indrah	mightily brave, he, o man, (is) Indra.

or, from the Bhadārayaka:

āpo vā arkah (= water, verily, fire) = water, yea, (*is*) fire

or:

tad yad apām šara (= that which of water on top) = that which of water (*was*) on top

Words formed from the root *bhū-* have a much different area of meaning from those of the Indo-European root *es- or from the simple expression of the copula (cf. *bhuta-* "being", *bhūtam* n. "being, creature", *bhavítram* "world", *bhū* "earth", bhúti- "well-being, good state (of health), growth, etc., "dwelling", bhúvanam n. "being, creature"). The nouns and adjectives which emerge from the root *bhū-* in Sanskrit show a distinct narrowing of meaning from the Indo-European "grow, flourish" toward the meaning "being (in time)." In distinction to the verb root *as-* this verb of being includes time as an essential element and thus also includes the notion of change in time. The nominal derivatives denote the animate aspects of existence, i.e., *being* as existing but also changing; *bhútam* and *bhúvanam* as a living being; *bhavitram* as the living world, *bhū* as the earth - ever changing.

In Sanskrit the use of one or the other of these verbs requires a choice in the meaning of being, that is, either with or without the inclusion of time. This is particularly significant in understanding texts in the Vedic literature, in particular those very few works in which there is speculation on the origins of being. These texts Rig Veda 10:129 and the second Brāhmane of the Brhad-Āranyaka Upanishad are of special importance.

Rig Veda 10,129 offers a particularly striking contrast in the semantic content of the two verbs which we are examining both in the forms which occur in this hymn and in their location within the verses. The forms are:
(The following numbers all refer to stanzas and lines of the Rig Veda text 10,129)

- *asati* instrumental singular case, non-being; one occurrence, 4,3
- *sat* n., nominative singular of the noun form of the present participle = being, one occurrence; 1,1
- *satas* n., genitive singular of the present participle; one occurrence, 1,1
- *āsīt*, third person singular preterit active indicative, eleven occurrences; 1,1 (twice); 1,2; 1,4; 2,1; 2,2; 3,1; 3,3; 4,2; 5,2 (twice)
- *āsan*, third person plural preterit active indicative of the verb (root *as*-); two occurrences; 5,3, in the sense of 'existed'.
- *āsa*, third person singular perfect active indicative; one occurrence; 2,4
- The forms from the verb root *as*-, i.e., the verb of being which does not contain the element of time, occur **only** in the first five stanzas of the hymn.

The forms from *bhū-,* i.e., the verb root with the element of time, occur only in the last two stanzas of the hymn where they have the meaning of 'come into being'. The forms of *as-* are absent in these two stanzas.

> *ā-babhūva*, third person singular perfect active indicative with the prefix **a-**giving the meaning "come into being", two occurrences; 6,4; 7,1

Within the larger context of the actual lines of verse:

1. <u>*Nāsad*</u> *āsin* nō sad *āsit* tadānīm <u>*nāsid*</u> rájo no vyomã paro yát/

1,1; the sense here is of being without the element of time
'there *existed* not non-being nor *existed* being then;
nor *existed* space nor sky beyond that'
nāsad = *na* (negation) + asat
asat n., nominative singular of the noun from the present participle not being; *nāsid.* One occurrence; *nāsid*; *na* = 'no' + *āsīt*; this is the simple past tense form of the verb *as-*.
nō = *na* 'not' + *u* 'and'
nāsad = na + asat, *a-* 'not' + *asat* 'non-being'

2. na mrtur *āsīd* amrtã na tarhi/
   na rātryā ahna *āsīt* praketatah

   'not *existed* death, nor non-death not there
   not (the) night-day *existed* phenomenon

   āsīt (twice), third person singular

3. táma *āsīt* támasā gūlham ágre/

praketám salilám sárvam ā idám/

'darkness *existed* in darkness concealed in the beginning/
indistinguishable flood all *this'*

again *asīt,* third person singular preterit active indicative

4. kāmas tad ágre sam avartādhī/

mánaso rétah prathamám yád *āsīt*/

'lust overcame this in the beginning.
whatever first seed of thought *existed,'*

āsīt, third person singular preterit active indicative

5. tirašcīno vitato rašmir eṣām/

adháh svid *āsīd* upari svid *āsīt*/

retodhā āsan mahiniāna *āsan*/

svadhā avastāt práyatih parástāt

'their line stretched horizontally.
whether something *existed* below,
whether (it) *existed* above.
(They) inseminating *existed,*
mighty beings *existed*, self-creations were above
inseminating downwards.'

āsīt, third person singular preterit active indicative; line 2 (twice)
āsan, third person plural preterit active indicative; line 3 (twice)

But, with the verb bhū-:

6. arvāg devā asyá visárjanenā-/
thā ko veda yáta *ābabhūva*

'Who knows whence it *came-into-being?'*

ābabhūva = *ā*+ *babhūva* perfect tense, 3rd person, singular of *bhū-*.

7. iyám visrṣṭir yáta *ābabhūva*/
yádi vā dadhé yádi vā ná/

'this creation whence it *came-into-being,'*

> The forms from the root *as-* occur in the first five stanzas only, while the forms from the root *bhū-* are confined to the final two stanzas where there are no occurrences of the *as-* root. Where the verb *bhu-* is accompanied by a predicate nominative it means "become", but without the predicate modifier as in this instance, it means only "being", but *being* in time as opposed to *being* as existing in the limited sense excluding time:
>
> *babhūva*, third person singular of the perfect tense gives the sense of 'has been and still is'. The prefix **ā-** adds the sense of 'arriving at, approaching' to the verb, but every prefix also adds the sense of perfected action, of completion.

as opposed to:
āsīt, third person singular preterit active indicative, "ex-

isted, was"

In the Brhad-Aranyaka Upanishad *bhū-* more frequently assumes the meaning of "become" while the root *as-* is far less frequently used and is usually absent where the subject has a noun or adjective modifier in the predicate. There is a clear transition in the meanings of the two verbs over the intervening four hundred years between the two texts during which interval the element of time included in the roo*t bhū-* has led to its use primarily in the sense of "become." This transition in meaning eventually led to the change in meaning of the Sanskrit verb *vartati* "turns" (= Latin *vertit)* to "is, being without time" in the later language.

The Vedic poet did not have the vocabulary to describe or name the incomprehensible but resolved this serious difficulty by describing what it was not, i.e., "not being and not not-being." In the last two stanzas of this Vedic hymn the time turns to the present where the verb of being becomes the verb, which also contains the semantic element of time, i.e., *bhū-*. In the first century AD, the Hindu philosopher Nagarjuna took up the question raised in this Vedic hymn and explored extensively the lexicon of thought on the origins of being using, for example, the word for 'emptiness' *šūunyā* "empty, void", *šūnyata* "emptiness, void" for the concepts left open with the Vedic use of the verbs of being and adding *anirodham* "non-ceasing, non-extinction", *anātman* "without self' Nagarjuna's approach appears to rely heavily on the manipulation of the semantic content of words, however, thus leaving unresolved the fundamental question of the origin of being. The answer does not lie in the lexicon but in overcoming the boundary between our reality and the incomprehensible - just as the poet of this Vedic text had understood a millennium earlier.

The existentialists of our own century have also sought within the meanings of words themselves the solution for the ultimate dilemma, the origin of existence. M. Heidegger's speculations in *Sein und Zeit* play with the meanings of words to an even greater extent than had Nagarjuna with the same inconclusive result. These thinkers have failed to grasp what the Vedic hymn saw in the inadequacy of language in explaining the inconceivable.

The occurrence of these two verbs of being in the Rig Veda can easily be followed and it is a simple task to examine and compare the usage as it occurs there. There is, however, a vast quantity of literature available to us from this very early period of Hindu thought (over 250,000 works from the first and second millennia BC) and desirable as it might be, it is virtually impossible to consider all the occurrences of the two in the entire body of literature. The difficulty here is compounded by the many different directions taken in Hindu thought in the millennia following the original hymns of the Rig Veda on questions of being and time. Students of Hindu thought from this earliest period have been particularly interested in following the emergence of particular aspects of Hindu religions and of the emergence of the various Hindu devas who populate the more recent religions of India. In order to focus specifically on the origin of ideas on being and time without regard for the particular aspects of the religions involved, it is simpler to choose those texts, which deal with the specific question. In particular, those very few works in which there is speculation on the origins of being, i.e., the texts: Rig Veda 10:129 and the second Brāhmana of the Brhad-Araṇyaka Upanishad as well as other books of the Upanishads.

The difference in meaning between the two verbs is particularly clear in contexts such as Rig Veda 5, 12, 5:

> sakhāyas te viṣuṇā agna ete šivāsah *santo* ašivā *abhūvan*
>
> 'These changing friends, Agni, are well disposed toward you (who) were ill disposed.'

Here we have an excellent example of the essential difference in meaning between the two verbs: *santo* (for *santas*, nominative plural of the present participle of *as* -) contrasts a state of being as an absolute where the grammatical present tense does not mean present time but indicates rather the absence of the element of time, this as opposed to the past tense form *abhavan* where the earlier inconstant condition is indicated through the use of the past tense form of *bhū-*. This verb thus denotes a state of being in which change can occur, i.e., being in time. The new state is not changeable, but permanent, i.e., it is absolute and this 'absoluteness' can only be indicated by the use of the verb of being which does not also contain the element of time.

For the use of the form of *bhū-* in Rig Veda 10, 129 has few parallels in the other hymns of the Rig Veda. There is only one other instance of the occurrence of the third person of the perfect tense with the prefix *ā-*:

> RV 10,168,3 (to Vāma, the storm wind)
> antarikse patibhir īyajāmano
> na ni viate katomac canāhah/
> apâ sakhā prathamajā
> rtāvā kva svij jātah kuta *ābabhūva*/

'Moving on paths in the sky,
(he) does not rest even a day.
He, companion of the waters, the first born,
the regular one, where (was he) born, or whence has he *come into being*?'

The forms of the Sanskrit root *bhū-* in the Rig Veda occur most frequently without any sort of prefix. The meaning of the unprefixed forms fall within the general semantic area of *be*, *become*, usually with the ėlement of time as the key semantic difference between this verb and the verb *as-*. Occasionally, however, the verb is all but indistinguishable from *as-* 'be', as in Rig Veda 7, 35, 7-13:

7. šã nah somo bhavatu brahma šã nah
šã no grāvānah šam u santu yajnāh |
šã nah svarūnām mitayo bhavantu
šã han prasvah šã v astu

8. šã nah sūrya urucakṣā ud etu
šã naš catasrah pradiṣo bhavantu |
šã nah parvatā dhruvayo bhavantu
šã nah sindhavah šã no santv āpah.

9. šã no aditir bhavatu vratebhih
šã no bhavantu marutah svarkāh
šã no vinuh šam u puṣā no astu
šã no bhavitram šam v astu vāyuh

10. šã no devah savitā trāyamānah
šã no bhavantūṣaso vibhātih |
šã nah parjanyo bhavatu prajābhyah
šã nah kṣetrasya patir astu šambhuh

11. šã no devā. višvadeva bhavantu

šã sarasvatī saha dhībhir astu
12. šam abhiṣācah šam u rātiṣācabh
šã no divyāh pārthivāh šã no apyah
13. šã nah satyasya patayo bhavantu
šã no arvantah šam u santu gāvah |
šã na rbhavah sukrtah suhastāh
šã no bhavantu pitaro haveṣu
14. šã no aja ekapād devo astu
šã no hr budhnyah ša samudrah |
šã no apã napāt perur astu šã
nah prnir bhavatu devagopā.

'May soma be good for us, may the Brahma be good for us, may the pressing stones (for soma) be good for us, may the sacrifices be good for us. May the erections of the ceremonial posts be good for us, may the grasses and the vedi be good for us. May the far seeing sun rise up well for us, may the four ends of the world be good for us. May the solid mountains be good for us, may the rivers and the waters be good for us. May the Aditi be good for us through their oaths, may the Maruts (the winds), the good singers, be good for us. May Vishnu be good for us, may Pushan be good for us; may the beings be good for us and the wind. May the protecting god Savitur be good for us, may radiant dawn be good for us. May Parjanya be good for our living beings, may the healing lord of the fields be good for us. May the gods be for good, the omni-deities, may Sarasvati be good for us through pious thoughts. May the companions and those who come with gifts be for good, may the heavenly and the earthly (beings) be good for us, good for us be those who dwell

> in the water. May the lords of truth be good for us, may racing horses be good for us, may the livestock be good for us, may the Ribhus who do good works with a good hand be good for us. May the fathers be good for us as they invoke. May the one-footed, unborn god be good for us, may the dragon of the deeps be good for us, may the sea be good for us. May the son of the waters be good for us, the impregnator, may Prishni, the protector of the gods, be good for us, Etc.

Here the third person singular and plural imperatives *astu, santu, bhavatu*, and *bhavantu* 'may he/she/it/they be' seem to be used with little attention to any fundamental difference in their meanings.

But the forms of the unprefixed perfect tense (third person singular), where they do occur, have the general meaning of 'come into being', as in:

RV 10,34,12
yo vah senānir mahato gaṇasya
rājā vrātasya prattamo *babhūva* |
tasmai krnami nadhanā ruṇadhmi
dašāham prācis ta rtam vadāmi ||

"Whoever is (*babhūva*, i.e., came to be and still is) the commander of your great army, to him I extend my ten (fingers) and swear an oath: I hold back no treasures."

An example of both the unprefixed imperative of the second person singular and perfect tense with the prefix *ā-* is to be found in RV 10,84,5:

viješakrd indra ivānavabravo
'smākam manyo adhipā *bhaveha* |
priyam te nama sahure grṇīmasi
vidmā tam utsam yata *ābabhūtha* ||

'A victory maker, Indra-like, not turning down,
be, Manyu, our defender here!
We praise your dear name, victor,
We know the source from which you came into being!'

bhaveha = *bhava* 'be' + *iha* 'here'
ābabhūtha = *ā* + *babhūtha* second person singular, active, indicative of the perfect tense

The imperative in this instance offers an additional example of the distinction between being in time as an ongoing, temporary state as contrasted with the absolute of *as-*, the other verb of being.

From the Chāndogya Upaniad VI 2,1 another version of the beginning of the world, but with a different take on its origin and a difference in opinion on the origin out of not-being:

1. *sad* eva somya idam agra *āsīd* ekam evādītīyam tadd haika āhuh *asad* evadam agra *āsīd* ekam evādvitīyā tasmād asatah *saj* jāyata.

   "(There) was being in the beginning, alone, without a second. Some say this, that in the beginning was not-being, alone, without a second and that from this being was born."

2. kutas tu khalu somya evā *syāt* iti hovāca, katham *asatah saj* jāyeteti, *sat* tu eva somya idam agra *āsīd*

ekam evādvitīyam.

"But how could this be", my lad, he said. "How could being be born of not-being. No, being was in the beginning, alone, without a second."

3. tad aikṣata. bahu *syā̃*. prajāyeti tat tejo 'srjata. Tat teja aikṣata. Bahu *syā̃* tat prajāyeti tad apo 'srjata tasmād yatra kvaca šocati svedate vā puruṣah tejasa eva tat adhyāpo jāyante.

It thought, "I would like to be many", and it created darkness. It thought, "I would like to be many" it created water. Therefore when it is hot or when some human sweats. From the warmth water is generated.

4. tā āpa aikṣata bahuvah *syāma*. prajāyemahīti. tā annam asrjanta. tasmād yatra kvaṣca varaṣti tat eva bhūyiṣṭan annā *bhavati*. adbhya eva tad adhyannādyā jāyate.

The water thought, "I would like to be many" it generated food. From this, when something rains, this becomes much food. From the water edible food is generated.

Here the distinction between *as-* and *bhavati* is maintained and the two are contrasted, but *bhavati* has now taken on much more the sense of *become*. The language of the Vedas is no longer the language of the Upanishads, it has continued the eternal process of change and in this process the meanings of the words of the hymn RV X 129 have also changed. The Hindus had, in fact observed that their language was changing in time and it was for this reason that they developed their unique tradition for memorizing and passing on the Vedic texts in such a way as to preserve the original sound patterns, but along with this they also developed a 'glossary' to retain the original meanings of the words of the Vedic texts. This did not, however, include the changes in the meanings of the words for being which we have been discussing. In the Brhad-Āranyaka Upanishad *bhū-* has assumed the meaning of "become" while the far less frequently occurring root *as-* is usually absent where the subject has a noun or adjective modifier in the predicate. The change in the meanings of the two verbs over the intervening four hundred years has some curious consequences: while the element of time included in the root *bhū-* has led to its use primarily in the sense of "become" and the sense of absolute being without the inclusion of time in the verb root *as-* seems to have been lost. This transition in meaning eventually led to the change in meaning of the Sanskrit verb *vartati* "turns" (= Latin *vertit*) to "is, being (without time)" in the later language. This now has created a change in the meaning of the hymn X 129 which could not have been detected by the authors of the texts of the Upanishads, but is never the less of significance in the subsequent deliberations on the nature of being as based on this very text, cf.

The difference between the notion of being with time and being without time is clearly defined here with the use of the two different verbs, but the inclusion or exclusion of time is never explicitly stated; there is no concept of time itself as an absolute concept.

The distinction between the two states of being, however, is crucial in understanding the significance of the argument in Chāndogya Upanishad VI 2,1ff. Where the origin of being out of not-being is rejected. Not-being (*asat*) is not just being without time in this statement; it is the absolute absence of being itself. The argument is thus: there is being without time from which being within time can be born. This draws on the concept of being without time which, however, has the potential of becoming being within time and thus allows the rejection of the concept of the absolute absence of being. The limitations of language in this instance has complicated the presentation of the argument since in the absence of the concept of time as an absolute entity there is no ready way to make the distinction between not-being as the complete absence of being and not-being as being without time, but with the potential for being within time. The argument relies instead on an expanded use of the two verbs of time to make the distinction and a newly introduced, but only implicit, distinction between not-being as the absolute absence of being in addition to being as being without time and being within time.

One can only marvel at the subtlety of thought of the early Hindu thinkers who confronted for the first time in human history the question of the origin of all being and of time. In western tradition the complexity of these questions was recognized by early Christian theologians and then more recently by philosophers, mathematicians, and physicists. In the early church tradition we find Augustine's speculations on time and the dilemma which the question poses[16]. The world, he offered, was made with time and not in time; time must be an essential aspect of the physical universe - of the creation - and the question of what was

---

[16]For this and the following comments see: P., C. W. Davies. *About time : Einstein's unfinished revolution.* New York: Simon & Schuster. 1995.

present before creation thus becomes pointless. Leibniz, on the other hand, was perplexed by the question of why god created the universe since he is in himself perfect and immutable. "For since God does nothing without reason and no reason can be given why He did not create the world sooner, it will follow either that He created nothing at all, or that He created the world before any assignable time, i.e., that the world is eternal."[17] Kant later rejected these possible solutions arguing that such a condition would require an infinite number of prior events or states of the world. But infinity can never be attained "by successive synthesis," and the notion of an eternal universe must thus be false. Nothing, however, can originate in "void time" as he called it, because "no part of any such time contains a distinctive condition of being, in preference to that of non-being." Most recently Stephen Hawking returned to the question of a "first event" which becomes moot in the general theory of relativity. If the universe was initially infinitely compressed ("Big Bang" theory) then it had a state of an infinite gravitational field, which represents an infinite warping of space-time. There is no continuation of space-time beyond this singularity.

With that first, profoundly disturbing line of Rig Veda X 129 the ancient Hindu kavi presented the world with an question which has since continued to haunt thinkers from all the world, and to us a dilemma which only in this century has found a tentative answer from western science. Beginning with Einstein's calculations on space and time and proceeding from there to Stephen Hawking's formulations that have served to remind us that in the onset of time *lies* the onset of *being*. To some extent this is much

[17]Ibid.

the conclusion offered by that ancient Vedic poet-thinker over three millennia ago, but where the conclusions of Einstein and Hawking are based on the language of mathematics - and are preceded by the work of many earlier mathematicians - the kavi drew his conclusions from language alone.

Certainly the ancient Hindu thinkers did not have anything comparable to contemporary western models of philosophical or mathematical argument at their disposal and it is at best difficult to compare the two traditions, but we must concede that their reasoning ultimately produced conclusions not unlike those of the western thinkers through their own unique approach to the question. And the reasoning in both traditions produces results, which are at best incomprehensible to us - though some, I suspect, believe, in their naiveté, that they do understand these perplexing ideas. For the people of that remote time these ideas could scarcely have been any more accessible or comprehensible than are the conclusions presented by contemporary thinkers, but they were never the less taken up and assimilated into the religion of the time and became an integral part of the subsequent developments in the religions of India.

The assimilation of these ideas into Hinduism presented a host of questions, which required resolution. Among these were questions about the immortality of the human 'soul.'

The Concept of the Life-Force
(It is usually mistranslated as Soul)

As we have seen in the previous chapters, the Rig Veda raised profound questions about *time* and *being*, particularly in the hymn X 127, to which the Vedic poets and seers sought answers. But in vain; the questions they raised cannot be answered. Yet this search continued into the *Brahmanas* and the *Upanishads* and has been taken up by successive generations of Indian thinkers since these sages first gave it their attention and the search goes on right up to the present time. But in the intervening centuries these brilliant thinkers, who were the first we know of to delve so profoundly into these impossible questions, have been gradually joined by thinkers from all over the world. The speculations on *time* and *being* raises other questions, however, foremost of which is the question about the nature of the vital force, that life force present in all living things. The speculations on *being* and *time* suggest that even the universe might not be permanent; all that exists must at some point cease its existence. If this is so, then that vital force must also be vulnerable, and must also perish only to be reborn and to enter into a cycle of rebirths or it must perish with all else never to return. The prospects presented in these ideas, however, run counter to the belief held by virtually all humans that the life force is immortal and survives into eternity. The belief that there is a part of man, which transcends life and continues living even after death is an ancient one that is common to all world cultures.

The Vedic hymns are the work of many different poets/seers from different times and places. Not constituting a single unified point of view, they present instead a whole spectrum of thought on a variety of questions. Likewise are the speculations of these poets/seers and of the thinkers whose ideas are passed on to us in the Brahmanas and the Upanishads. None constitute a single, unique, coherent view of the nature of the vital force, but are rather the speculations of individual thinkers on this subject. As such they represent the incredibly sophisticated thoughts of a number of wise men of the time, who were dealing with ideas that continue to defy satisfactory resolution. For any serious attempt to examine Indian thought on the nature of the vital force this presents a difficult challenge.

> *... To die, to sleep;*
> *To sleep, perchance to dream: ay there's the rub;*
> *For what dreams may come when we have shuffled off this mortal coil,*
> *Must give us pause. There's the respect that makes calamity of so long life;*
>
> *Shakespeare*: *Hamlet* III, I 56.

Death poses two essentially unrelated problems for the survivors that become intertwined with beliefs (which we call superstitions when speaking of the customs of other peoples) about the nature of death. First, there is the usually urgent need, to make some disposition of the mortal remains of the recently departed. And then there remains the question of what has become of that life force which only recently was so apparent in what has now become a lifeless object.

The development of the concept of the vital force, the life force in all beings, that which survives all cycles of birth and rebirth, in the oldest Sanskrit sources follows from the Vedic speculations on the nature of being and time, and form the basis for later thought on the nature of that vital force. If the universe is created, then the vital force is a part of this creation and must suffer the same fate as the creation. If the coming into being of the universe is an eternal process of birth, death, and rebirth then the vital force must be a part of this process, i.e., it, too, must come into being out of that process and as a part of the process.

As one of the concepts of being and time, which we covered in the first part of this essay, we find the notion of the cyclical annihilation and return of the universe with the implication that all that exists must perish before this rebirth. This would seem to negate any suggestion of an eternal 'soul' with its attendant notion of the soul as a continuation of the essential nature of the individual. The beliefs of the culture, however, lie outside the speculations of the ancient kavi, but we see emerging even at this very early time in the history of Hindu thought the belief in an individuated vital force along side the vital force as a part of a greater life force to which it ultimately returns. This latter belief tends toward a virtually atheistic perception of a vital force which will pass through the cyclical process without a continuing knowledge of its many reincarnations just as the devas pass through a similar process of endless reincarnations without any creator or creative force. Given the numerous interpretations which are to be found in today's Eastern religions it strikes me as all but impossible to catalog each or even several of the vast variety of beliefs.

Whatever the early speculations about the nature of being and time may have been, they are never really directed toward the other immediate problem posed by death, i.e., what to do with the mortal remains. Here is the question of the connection between what was once the dwelling of the vital force and the vital force itself impinging on the question of how to dispose of what is left after the vital force has departed.

The funeral rites of different cultures and the varying rites even within cultures are the reflection of the answers, which peoples everywhere have found to these problems. Inhumation and cremation involve the removal of the mortal remains, but they also involve always some concept about what has become of the departed life force. Inhumation may hold the implicit belief in a resurrection of the body and the restoration of the life force. Burials in cairns or mausoleums, which we find in many parts of the world, may arise from the belief that the life force is still present somewhere nearby and will eventually return. In keeping with this belief the burial site may even hold equipment for the anticipated continuation of life. This can go so far as the placement of utensils for dining and entertainment or for the continuation of the work which the deceased had pursued during his lifetime; work including the implements of war. Even possessions of the departed, such as servants and animals, which might be useful in this continuation of life, are found often in gravesites from cultures everywhere and through all history. The possibilities seem virtually endless and the customs we know of from various parts of the world provide a never-ending parade of beliefs and practices.

Oftentimes the departed life force is thought of as lingering somewhere in the vicinity of its former dwelling or near the place of death, perhaps in the dwellings of the relatives of the departed or in some sacred place - a dedicated spot or shrine, for example. To placate these 'spirits' the living and especially the relatives of the deceased may provide a daily ration of food, which is usually placed in a household shrine. But routine offerings may not suffice if there is concern that the lingering spirit may actually be harmful; this may require the services of an expert to rid the premises of a malicious, malevolent presence.

In India the funeral practices common among Hindus and among the religions deriving from the same sources as Hinduism or from closely related sources certainly did not begin with Hindu thinkers as did the concepts of being and time which we discussed earlier, but derive, certainly, from ancient customs and beliefs about the nature of death. These beliefs and practices may have come in part from the Indo-European source, but it must be clear that many beliefs and practices have also been introduced from the indigenous cultures or from neighboring cultures of ancient India. The funeral customs display many different forms even within the several branches of the Hindu religion. E.g.: premise

In his *Hinduismus* (1922) Helmuth von Glasenapp describes a Hindu funeral/cremation:[1]

---

[1]"Wenn ein Hindu seinen Tod kommen sieht, so spricht er nach Möglichkeit heilige Sprüche, um sein zukünftiges Leben angenehm zu gestalten. Bald nachdem der Tod eingetreten ist, wird der Leichnam nach der meist in der Nähe eines heligen Flusses gelegenen Verbrennungstätte gebracht. Dort wird er auf einem Scheiterhaufen verbrannt. Wenn die Verbrennung sich ilirem Ende nähert, wird der Schadel des Toten durch einen Schlag mit geweihtem Holze gespalten, um der Seele ihren Austritt aus dem Leibe zu erleichtern. Nach vier Tagen werden dann die überreste gesammelt und in den Fluß geworfen. In früheren Zeiten geschah es mitunter, daß sich die Witwe mit ihrem verstorbenen Gatten zusammen verbrennen ließ. Diese Sitte findet sich zuerst in den jüngeren Rechtsbüchern und den großen Epen, ist jedoch dem Veda noch fremd, wenn die Brahmanen sie freilich auch später in ihn hineinzulegen versuchten. Der leitende Gedanke, der viele Witwen dazu veranlaßte, ihrem entseelten Gatten in die andere Welt zu folgen, war der Wunsch, dem Gemah als eine gute Frau („Sati") die Treue auch über den Tod hinaus zu halten. Ganz außerordentlich ist der Lohn, der einer solchen Gattin in Aussicht gestellt

"When a Hindu sees death approaching, he begins to speak sacred words as much as possible in order to give a pleasant form to his future life. Shortly after death has intruded, the body is usually carried to the cremation site, which is usually located in the vicinity of a nearby stream or river. There it is cremated on a funeral pyre. When the cremation has almost reached its end the skull of the deceased is shattered with a hallowed wooden stick in order to ease the soul's exit from the body. After four days the remains are gathered up and thrown into the river. In earlier times it happened occasionally that the widow had herself cremated together with her departed husband. This custom is to be found only in more recent law books and in the major epics, but it is unknown in the Vedas, even though the Brahmans have tried to work it into the Vedas. The primary thought which prompted many widows to follow their departed husbands into the next world was the desire as a good wife ('sati') to maintain her allegiance even beyond death. The reward, which awaits such a wife, is quite extraordinary.

In a passage from Cānakyas he says:

'If, in order to accompany her husband,
a wife would go to the funeral pyre,
verily each of her steps gains her a reward

---

wurde. In einem Spruche Cānakyas heißt es darüber:

'Wenn ihren toten Gatten zu begleiten,

Die Gattin will zum Scheiterhaufen schreiten, Erwirbt ihr jeder Schritt den Lohn fürwahr,

Als brächte sie ein Pferdeopfer dar.'"

as if she were presenting a sacrificial offering.'."

The sacred words to which von Glasenapp refers are usually the repetition of the sacred syllable Om. Should this prove to be the last syllable spoken by the dying person then immediate release (Sanskrit *moka*) from the endless cycle of rebirths ensues. (Bhagavadgita 8,6)

This belief is to be found in Bhagavadgita, 8, 1ff.:

Šri bhagavān uvaca: *akṣarā brahma paramā* *svabhāvo 'dhyātmam ucyate* *bhūtabhāvodbhavakaro* *visargah karmasājñitah*	The Lord said: I am Akshara Brahma, the ultimate, by nature I am called the supreme ātman, existing in all beings, known as Karma creating (all beings).
adhibūtā kṣaro bhāvah *purṣuašcā* *'dhidaivatam* *adhiyajño 'ham evā 'tra* *dehe dehabhrtā vara.*	Adhibūta *I am* called, being material, perishable things, and Purusha *being* spiritual, *I am* Adhiyajna the lord of the sacrifice here, in the body embodied enclosing.
antakāle ca mām eva *smaran muktvā kalevaram* *yah prayāti sa madbhāvam* *yāti nā'sty atra sāšayah*	Whoever leaves his body in the final hour remembering me attains my abode. There is no doubt about this.

yã yã vā 'pi smaran bhāvam tyajaty ante kalevaram tã tã evaiti kaunteya sadā tadbhāvabhāvitah sadā tadbhāvabhāviah	While remembering whatever thing as one leaves the body at the end of life, one attains that object, Arjuna!, because of the constant thought of that object.
tasmāt sarveṣu kāleṣu mām anusmara yudhya ca mayy arpitamanobud-dhir mām evai 'yasy asãšayam	Therefore, at all times remember me and do your battle for (me). You shall certainly attain me if your mind and intellect are fixed on me.
abhyāsayogayuktena cetasā nā 'nyagāminā paramã puruã divyã y āti pārthā 'nucintayan	By contemplating me with unwavering mind, disciplined by the practice of meditation, one attains the Supreme Being, Arjuna!
kavim purāṇam anušāsitāram aor aiyãsam anus-mared yah sarvasya dhātāram acintyarūpam ādityavarã tamasah parastāt	Whoever thinking on the most ancient seer, instructor, smallest of the small, giver of all, the inconceivable, the sun-colored, beyond *the* darkness, etc…

According to age, sex, and family relationship the survivors are considered 'unclean' for prescribed periods.

In general the mourning period for Brahmans days, for a Kshatriya it is 12 days, for a Vaisya 14, and for a Sudra 31. During this time the survivors provide sacrificial offerings for the deceased and at the end of the period they must undergo a purification ceremony.

Within the month after the death the son of the deceased or someone who can take the place of the son must hold a celebration for the deceased. The celebration includes presentation of rice-balls to the household deities and he is to provide food and gifts for the mourners and the Brahmans who are the representatives of the ancestors. The celebration is repeated from time to time later on a smaller scale[2].

The remains of ascetics and holy men are not burned, but buried and the gravesites of the noted holy men become pilgrimage sites for the faithful.

The Vedic sources indicate that inhumation was the accepted funeral practice of the earlier period. Why this practice changed in the later Brahman and Hindi times is not at all clear. More to the point, it is not clear what expectations might be ascribed to present day funeral practices of the Hindus or from the practices of the earlier Vedic period.

In India, among Hindus, cremation is the preferred path and devout Hindus all share the hope of being incinerated in Varanasi. Here the banks of the river are lined with concrete and marble platforms on which funeral pyres can be erected. The remains are then scattered in the Ganges River.

On the small Indonesian island of Bali cremation ceremonies are a survival of the influence of the ancient oc-

---

[2]Helmuth von Glasenapp. *Der Hinduismus. Religion und Gesellschaft im heutigen Indien*. München: Kurt Wolf Verlag. 1922.

cupation of this island region from India, but elements of the indigenous animistic religion of the region have been incorporated into the foreign practices. The dead are initially laid out in the dwelling of the relatives for a week where family, friends and members of the community can visit. After one week the body is usually temporarily interred until the time when the preparations for the cremation can be carried out. The celebration is costly and it can take several years for the family to accumulate enough wealth to meet the expenses of the celebration. The actual preparations include the construction of an elaborate, high, gold decorated tower of wood and bamboo and a black water buffalo also of wood and bamboo in which the body will be cremated. To save on costs, as many as four or five bodies may be placed in this wooden container and all are cremated together. The construction of the tower and of the black water buffalo is also complicated by the requirement that it proceed only on days when the portents are promising so that attendant spirits will not be offended. The cremation must also be carried out on a day for which the portents are good and the celebration itself is an occasion for great joy. There is a colorful procession with the tower and the black water buffalo all of which is accompanied by much merriment as the bearers of the two objects turn their burdens about in the streets in order to confuse any spirits which might accompany the bodies to the site of the cremation so that they will not find their way back to the dwelling of the deceased. After the cremation - which must take place on the shores of a body of water - the ashes are scattered over the water and the celebrants move on to the festive activities, which may continue for several days. In some regions there follows a period of forty-two days after which a second tower, with effigies instead of bodies, is burned. This will aid the vital force of the departed as it proceeds on its long journey. The ashes of the towers, like those of the bodies, are scattered on the water.

The Afterlife

We find already in Vedic sources the recognition of a realm of the dead with its ruler Yama[3] who becomes its deva. This perpetuates the traditional beliefs of the original Aryan population and does not begin to come to terms with the newly advanced concepts on the nature of being and time. In the course of the subsequent generations of Hindu thinkers, however, it assumes the traditional beliefs are incorporated into the development of concepts of an afterlife, eventually expanding on the belief in a realm of the dead expressed in the Rig Veda, in which one finds the misdeeds of this life punished or rewarded. The ruler of this Vedic realm of the dead is **Yama**. As Edmund Hardy pointed out early in this century[4]: "*Für die Formen des religiösen Glaubens und Brauches gibt es nur eine Erklärung: das Herkommen. Wie der Vater, so der Sohn. Aber es geht keineswegs das väterliche Erbe unverändert durch des Sohnes Hände . . . Der Glaube, daß das Jenseits die nächste Hülle Wohnort der abgeschiedenen Seelen (nicht der Bösen zur Strafe), ein Glaube, den die arischen Inder einst vollkommen natürlich fanden, hat in der uns sugänglichen Periode seine Lebenskraft verloren. In lichter Himmelsregion wohnen die "Väter" zusammen mit Yama, dem Totengott.*"

---

[3]Yama: v. illustration, p. 11.

[4]Hardy, Edmund. Indische Religionsgeschichte. Leipzig: G. J. Göschen'sche Verlagshandlung. 1904

The name of this deva, Yama, goes back to the Indo-European root **yem-* 'hold, hold together, to couple, copulate; compel.' From this root comes Sanskrit *yama-* 'twin' which in turn is also related to the Sanskrit verb *ya-mati* 'drive, rein'. It is further akin to Latin *geminus* 'twin, doubled' and to the Old Norse deity *Ymir*, the giant from whose body man was generated. The original meaning of twin also allows for the concept of the hermaphrodite, which can reproduce from itself, and this meaning underlies the Sanskrit name.

Yama, in the Rig Veda means 'pair' or twins (particularly the Asvins as twin sisters). Yama then appears later with *Yami* (as *Yama* and *Yami)*, the first pair of twins; they are called the offspring of the Gandharva and the Water-maiden (Rig Veda X 10, 4). In other hymns Yama is called the son of Vishvavat and Saranyu (Rig Veda X 17, 1) "[Saranyu] ...the mother of Yama, the ...wife of Vishvavat." He appears then with the patronymic *Vevasvata* and as the father of mankind. In Rig Veda X 135, 1, Yama is the one to whom the blessed spirits of the dead return and he provides them with their home "Where Yama drinks together with the devas under a leafy tree, there our progenitor, (our) father, seeks the ancestors." And, as one of the devas who drinks together with other devas under the leafy tree "This is the seat of Yama which is called the palace of the devas... "(ib. 7). He is worshiped as a deva especially with Varuna (Rig Veda X 14, 7)"Go, go . . . where you see the two kings, Varua and Yama enjoying themselves." And with Brhaspati (X 13, 4; X 14, 3) "They (the devas) made the rishi Brhaspati their sacrifice; Yama removed his dear body." He is placed on an equal footing with Agni in Rig Veda I 66, 8: "(Agni) Yama born, Yama to be born, the lover of maidens, husband of women." And in Rig Veda I

164, 46: " . . . those who speak well often name (them). They say Agni, Yama, Matarishvan." In Rig Veda X 165, 4 Yama is explicitly the deva of Death: "Let it be of no consequence what the owl cries, and even when the dove sets her foot on the fire. Let one make obeisance to him whose messenger it is, to this Yama, to Death (*mrtyave*)." But the view of Yama's realm as the place where Yama "drinks together with the devas under a leafy tree" later becomes one of a place in which the dead are punished for their misdeeds in life or rewarded (with treatment appropriate to this earlier verse), but all these beliefs follow easily from the picture which emerges from the Vedas.

The road to Yama is the path to death: (Rig Veda) I 38, 5 "Let not your singer be dissatisfied like the wild animal in the field nor arrive on Yama's path."; or death as a fetter: (Rig Veda X 97, 16) "Let them free me from . . . and from Yama's fetters and from any sin against the devas."

Yama's realm and the path leading to it are guarded by two four-eyed, broad nosed hounds that prohibit the godless from passing between them. (Rig Veda X 14, 10 - 12): 10, "Run past the four-eyed, spotted, Saramaic watchdog pair on the right path, and go to the fathers who are easy to find, who enjoy the shared meal with Yama."; 11, "Your two dogs, Yama, four-eyed watchdogs guarding the path, they with commanding eyes, to them I entrust him, O king, and give him fortune and happiness."; 12, "These two broad-nosed . . . go as Yama's messengers among us."

The Upanishads and the concepts of death and afterlife

It is centuries later in the Upanishads the attempts at

reconciling the discrepancies between concepts of the fate of the vital force and that of being, i.e., of the cycle of birth and death of the universe, the origin of the universe out of nothing, or of the creation of the universe and all that it contains by a specific deva (Brahma) gradually began to appear. But, as Balbir Singh explains[5], "What does not, however, fit into the Upanishadic metaphysical framework was the cult of ritualism prevalent and practiced in that age. If the object of the quest is the universal Self, sacrifices and offerings were too inadequate to take the aged to the accepted goal. All these were generally motivated by some mundane consideration and were, therefore, selfish at bottom. In most cases rites and sacrifices were performed with a view to the attainment of heaven (svarga-prāpti). This, in the eyes of the Upanishadic philosophers, was not the highest goal..." The explanations which the Upanishads offer are based on profound philosophical speculations and differ significantly from the popular views of that time and still of the popularly held views today.

In the Brhadaranyaka we find a discussion of the vital force, which begins the explanation of, that which does not perish, but survives after death. The traditional belief in the immortality of the vital force and some belief in the retention of individual identity is retained as the vital force continues its existence. The explanations begin with the question of what becomes of the vital force after it has departed the body. This question, however, demands a definition of the vital force, i.e., what is it and how does it survive? The answers - for the future thinkers, in particular - depend on the explanation on the origin of being, of the

[5]Balbir Singh. *The Philosophy of the Upanishads.* Atlantic Highlands, NJ: Humanities Press Inc. 1983.

universe and all that it contains. If it is created then it may come to an end only to be created again, or, if it is a part of a cycle of birth, death, and rebirth, an essentially atheistic concept, then it will come into being grow, perish, and be reborn. But, what becomes of the vital force in this process? The Upanishads - like the Rig Veda - are not the work of a single original thinker, but the compilation of the thoughts of several independent thinkers who present, each, their own unique explanations which move in the different directions according to the fundamental concept of being espoused by the individual. Does the vital force survive its release from the body? Does the vital force retain its individual identity, its knowledge?

Of the Upanishads one in particular, the Kaha Upanishad, makes use of Yama, the deva of the dead, who is alternately addressed as Yama or Death, to explore the question of what becomes of the departed vital force. The question is posed by Naciketa, dutiful son of Vājaśrava, who has annoyed his father with some criticism of his less than generous sacrificial offerings. In his anger the father condemns Naciketa to Yama's realm, i.e., to death[6]. Too late Vājaśrava regrets his action, but Naciketa goes to Yama obeying his father's rash command. Yama is delayed for three days in greeting his guest, but responding as the gracious host that he is, grants Naciketa three wishes - one for each day of delay. As his third wish Naciketa asks for an answer to that most perplexing question:

yeyā prete vicikṣitsā manuye 'stīti eke nāyam

[6]An excellent, detailed exposition of this text is to be found in Sw□m□ Nikhilananda. *Man in Search of Immortality*. London : George Allen and Unwin. 1968.

astīti caike etat vidyām anušiṣṭas tvayāhā varām eṣ varas trtīyah.

Some [say] that when the mind has departed it is gone, some that this is not so. This (i.e., the answer to this), as my third wish, I would like to know from you.

Naciketa does not want to know whether the vital force continues its existence after departing, but whether it continues its existence as an individual having left its mortal abode; the continued existence of the vital force is a given and Naciketa had already said earlier that:

anupašya yathā pūrve pratipašya tathāpa re sasyam iva martyah pacyate sasyam iva jāyate maryah.

See! Just as it was, lo, so it shall be in the future. Like grain, a mortal ripens and like grain he is born again.

Thus recognizing the endless cycle of rebirths. But here Naciketa wants to know whether the vital force retains its individual identity. Yama/Death explains that even the devas are not in agreement on this. In a series of carefully reasoned steps Yama explains that in this world there are many men who seek only pleasure while others seek good. Those who seek the pleasures of this world are condemned to return again and again to this world, but those who seek good will find release from the cycle of rebirths and become absorbed into the

> Brahma/the *ātman* or the vipašcin = the supreme being which, as Yama explains:
>
> najayāate mryate vā vipašcin nāyam kutašcin na babhūva kašcit ajo nityah šašvato 'yam purāno no hanyate kanyamāne šarire.
>
> The vipašcin is not born, does not die, does not come from anywhere, nor does not become anything. He is unborn, eternal, ancient, not slain when the body is slain.

And the *ātman*/Brahman/vipašcin is everywhere, is everything. Kaha Upanishad I 2, 20:

> aṇor aṇīyām mahato mahīyān ātmāsya jantor nihito guhāyā: tam akratuh pašyati vītašoko dhātu prasādā mahinānam āmanah.
>
> Smaller than the smallest larger than the largest the *ātman* of each creature is concealed: the man free of desire, free of sorrow sees him. By tranquility of the mind he sees the magnitude of the *ātman*.

What is the vital force?

But what is this vital force? The Hindu thinkers use the terms *prāṇāh* and *ātman-* for the 'vital force', which in the Rig Veda meant 'breath' or 'wind' as well as 'vital force'. They appear to create here a distinction between the vital force as an absolute and the vital force as the essence of the individual being and even of the whole of the spiritual aspect of the individual, his knowledge and his virtues and faults.

But the origins of the belief in an after-life and the association of breath with the vital force which does not perish with the body are far older than the Vedic (Sanskrit) tradition. The Sanskrit words which we have traditionally translated as 'soul' are inherited from the mother tongue, i.e., from Indo-European where their meanings differ only slightly from that found in the Hindu texts.

The roots of the Sanskrit terms for the vital force, i.e., *prāṇāh* and *ātman-* (Both with the meaning of the vital force):

The former comes from the Indo-European root *an-* 'breathe'; which in Sanskrit has the verb form: *aniti* 'breathes', and, also, the thematic form (i.e., the vowel *-a-*is inserted between the verb root and the verb endings) *anati*; from this same root we also find the nouns *anila-* 'breath, wind'; *prāṇiti* (with the prefix *pra-* i.e. *pra-anā-* yields *prāṇ-*) 'breathes.' From this is derived the noun *prāṇāh* 'breath, vital force.'

In Greek this Indo-European root appears in words like: ἄνεμος 'breath, wind' and in Latin it is found in the word *animus* 'spirit, soul', *anima* 'breath, breath of air, soul, life'.

Old Irish knows the form *anāl*, Cymric *anall* 'breath'; while the Germanic languages know it in words such as Gothic (a Germanic language attested in Bishop Ulfila's 4th century translation of the Holy Bible) *uz-anan* 'exhale', and (with the -t formation): Old Norse (one of the North Germanic languages) has this root in the form and (genitive *andar*) 'breath, life, soul', *anda* 'breathe': The related West Germanic language Old English has *óðian* 'blow hard (puff)' closely resembling the Old Norse *andi* 'breath, spirit, soul'.

The Slavic languages also have forms of this root as in Old Bulgarian *vonja* (< *aniā*) 'odor'.

Tocharian A and B *āñm-* 'life, spirit', Tocharian B āñme 'intent' Tocharian A *āñ*cäm 'life, spirit'.

The other Sanskrit word, which also becomes a term referring to the vital force is found in Vedic *ātman-* (genitive: *ātmanah*) m. 'breath, soul'. This is the Indo-European root which we find in Old English *œđm* masc. Old Saxon *āthum* 'breath', Old High German *ātum* 'breath'.

The development of the meanings of *prāṇāh* and ā*tman-* in later Sanskrit

The terms which from the time of the Rig Veda to the end of the period of the Upanishads, gradually take on the meaning of 'vital force' as they evolve from their original meanings of 'spirit, air (in motion)' complicate the discussion of the early Hindu concept of the vital, life force since the changes, though significant, are gradual and subtle. The following pages will provide an overview of these changes and clarify to some extent the emergence of the new meanings.

In the Vedic forms of these terms we see primarily their original meaning of 'breath' or 'wind', as movement of air and in many contexts it is even equated with the word for *wind* or *breeze*. For example:

ātmā, in the basic meaning of breath, breeze, is seen most clearly in the comparison with Sanskrit *vāta* (I 34,7;

VII 87, 2; X 168, 4; X 92, 13). Closely related to these is the meaning *life's breath* and subsequently with the meaning of *vital force, basis of life.* This extends even to the sense in which it is used in speaking of the essential force of illness (yáksmasya), which is found in Rig Veda X 97, 11.

In one place, however, (Rig Veda, IX 113,1) **ātmā** refers to the actual living body in a way which foreshadows the later development of its use as a reflexive pronoun 'self' (s. below). The words which appear in the later Brahmanas and the Upanishads in the meaning of the vital force (**prāṇá** and **ātmā**) do not have this exclusive sense in the Rig Vedas, where we can only observe the beginning of the change in meaning from the various contexts in which the two words occur.

Vedic **prāṇá**- masculine, [derived from the root *an*- with the prefix pra-] has the meanings 1) breath, breathing, puff of air, and 2) life's Vital Force.

Examples:

Rig Veda I 66, 1	*rayir na citrā sūro na sãdrg āyur na* ***prāṇo*** *nityo na sūnuh* like wealth, like the bright face of the sun, like **prāṇá**, like one's own son
Rig Veda III 53, 21	*yo no dvety adharah sas padīṣṭa yam u dvinas tam u* *prāṇo jahātu.* whoever is (our) enemy may he fall, whomever we have as enemy, may his **prāṇá** depart
X 59, 6	*asunīte punar asmāsu cakṣuh punah*

	***prāṇám** iha no dhehi bhogam,* Asunite! (give) us again the eye (sun), again the **prāṇá** here below, and the pleasure,

But: prāṇá- in the meaning breath, breath of Air:

Rig Veda X 90, 13	*mukhād indraš cāgniš̌ca **prāṇād** vāyur ajāyata* from (his, i.e., purusha) mouth Indra and Agni (came), from his **prāṇá**, the wind.
Rig Veda X 189, 2	*antaš carati rocanāsyá **prāṇād** apānati.* He goes in the bright sky, breathing from his **prāṇá**

Ātmā in the Vedic text also has some slightly different meanings.

Examples:

In the basic meaning of air flow, breath of air:

Rig Veda I 34,7;	*...tisró nāsatyā rathyā parāvāta **ātm**eva vātah svasarai gacchatam.* 'three distances you Nasatya's charioteers come here to the morning ritual wind breath-like
Rig Veda VII 87, 2;	*. . . **ātmā** te vāto raja ā navīnot paṣur na bhūrnir yavase sasavān . . .* your breath rustles fiery in space like an animal victorious on the meadow
Rig Veda X 168, 4	*...**ātmā** devānām bhuvanasya garbho yathāvaṣā carati deva ešah*

	. . . the **ātmā** of the gods, the child of the world, this deva, goes about as he will . . .
Rig Veda X 92, 13	*pra nah pūṣā carathā viśvadevyo 'pā napād avatu vāyur iṣṭaye, ātāmanā vasyo abhi vātam arcata tad aśvinā su-havā yāmani śrutam.* may Pusha, friend of the devas, make our path easy, Apam, Napat, Vayu, so that we quickly arrive at our goal.

Meaning breath, life's breath:

Rig Veda I 162, 20	*mā tvā tapat priya* ***ātmā****piyantan ma svadhitis tanva a tiṣṭhipat te,* precious **ātmā** should not cause you to suffer when you perish,
Rig Veda I 164, 4	*bhumya asur asrg* ***ātmā*** *kva svit ko vid-vsam upa gat praṣṭum etat.* where, then, is the earth's **ātmā**, breath, blood, ...
Rig Veda VIII 3, 24	***ātmā*** *pitus tanūr vāsa ojodā ab-hyañjanam,* **ātmā** is the nourishment, the body, the cloak, the salving oil is the strength giv-ing enhancement
Rig Veda X 16, 3	*sūryam cakṣur gacchatu vātam* ***ātmā*** *dyām ca gaccha prthivim ca dharmaā* into the sun let your eye go, let the **ātmā** (go) into the wind, go into the sky and the earth as is right!
Rig Veda I 163, 6	***ātmānā*** *te manasārād ajānām avo divā patayantam patāgam,* In my mind your own **ātmā** I recognized

	from afar, the bird flying below the sky
Rog Veda X 97, 4	*saneyam ašvã gã vāsa* ***ātmānã*** *tava pūruṣa.*
	O man! I would like to gain horse, cow, clothing, and **ātmā** from you.
and X 97, 8	*dhanã saniyantīnām* ***ātmānã*** *tava puruṣa*
	O man! (they) would like to gain wealth and **ātmā** from you.
Rig Veda X 163, 5, and 6.	*yakmã sarvasmād* ***ātmānas*** *tam idã vi vrhãmi te*
	(this) pervasive illness I take now from all of your **ātmā**

ātmā appears as the essential, vital force of life:

Rig Veda I 115, 1	*āprā dyavāprthivī antarikṣ sūrya* ***ātmā*** *jagatas tasthuṣaš ca*
	filling heaven and earth, the sky, the sun the **ātmā** of whatever moves and stands
Rig Veda VII 101, 6	*sa retodā vrṣabhah šašvatīnām tasminn* ***ātmā*** *jagatas tathuṣ aš ca,*
	He, the semen giving bull of all dawns, in him is the **ātmā** of whatever moves and stands
Rig Veda X 107, 7	*dakṣiānnā vanute yo na* ***ātmā*** *daki varma krṇnute vijānan*
	the dakshina gives food which is our **ātmā**, the one who knows asks the dakshina his protection (Soma as the basic life force of the sacrifice, of Indra.)
Rig Veda IX 2, 10	*goša indo nrṣa asy avasa vājasa uta,* ***ātma*** *yajñasya purvyah.*

(to Soma) bright droplets! you are the bringer of cattle, bringer of men, of horses, and of strength, the first **ātmā** of the sacrifice

Rig Veda IX 6, 8 ***ātmā*** *yajñasya ranhyā suṣyāṇah pavate sutah, pratanā ni pāti kāvyam.*

ātmā (Soma) of the sacrifice, quickly pressed the pressed (liquid) clarifies, protects the ancient wisdom of the seers.

Rig Veda IX 85, 3 *adabdha indo pavase madintama ātmendrasya bhavasi dhāsir uttamah,*

pure, bright droplets, you become clarified, o most intoxicating one! You become Indra's **ātmā**, (his) highest achievement.

And once **ātmā** is used in the meaning of the vital force of a disease

(yakshmasya):X 97,11yad imā vājayann aham oṣadhīr hasta ādadhe, **ātmā** yakṣmasya našyati purā jīvagrbho yathā

When I take the prize with (the) herbs in hand, (my)

ātmā of the pervasive illness perishes as before something seizing living things.

5) And as the living body, the self - reflexive pronoun:

Rig Veda I 73, 2 *purupraṣasto amatir na satya* ***ātm****eva ševo didhiṣayyo bhūt*

praised by many, truly precious as his own self (**ātmā**), who should be sought after

Rig Veda IX 113, 1 *balā dadhāna* ***ātmāni*** *kariṣyan vīryam mahad indrāyendo pari srava.*
getting strength for **ātmā** (himself) going to commit a great deed of courage. For Indra flow, bright droplets! (Indra will gain great strength through the drink of Soma).

Finally, in classical Sanskrit this word also takes on the meaning of 'self' as a reflexive pronoun indicating that its meaning of 'vital force' also included the sense of the vital force which bears the identity of the individual. E.g., from classical Sanskrit we find, ***ātmānā*** *sā hanti* 'she struck herself', and many other such occurrences.

Thus the terms *ātmā* and *prāṇá* have in the Vedic texts only the meanings 'breath' and 'vital force' while the term *ātmā* also begins to hint at the later additional meaning, the reflexive pronoun 'self'. The difficulty in translating these terms into other languages has already been touched on in the first part of this study, but they present an even greater problem in the discussion of this concept of the vital force. In a book titled *Self as Person in Asian Theory and Practice* Wimal Dissanayake[7] elects to translate the Sanskrit word *ātma* with the English word 'self' which is a fairly common translation of this term in English texts. Other translators prefer 'soul' and a few choose, as I have done, the expression 'vital force' or 'life force.' 'Self' and 'soul', however, suggest the differentiated, individualized life force and this does seem to be excluded in the Upani-

---

[7]Dissanayake, Wimal. Introduction to Part Four. In: *Self as Person in Asian Theory and Practice*; Ed. Roger T. Ames with Wimal Dissanayake & Thomsa P. Kasulis. Albany, NY: State University of New York press. 1994.

shad passages where the dissolution of the individual *ātmā* in the all pervasive universal *ātmā* is likened to the rivers flowing into the sea or the honey collected by the bees as losing their individual identity, their knowledge of who they are or whence they came. In the example of the tree of which the branches may perish individually while the tree still remains 'alive' it is the departure of the *ātmā* which ultimately signifies the death of the tree itself. Here the translation 'soul' or 'self' scarcely seems appropriate[8]. Either the 'vital force', the force which provides life to the otherwise inanimate body, or simply the Sanskrit '*ātmā*' seems to provide a more satisfactory translation.

Does the vital force survive its escape from the body?

In the Brhadaranyaka the preeminent Hindu thinker Yajñavalkya responds with a question of his own to a question inspired by Videha King Janaka who desires instruction: "Where will you go when released *from this body*?" asks Yajñavalkya.

Brhadaranyaka IV 2, 4

1. *janako ha vaidehah kūrcād upāvasarpann uvāca: namas te 'stu yājñavalkya, anu mā šādhīti. sa hovāca: yathā vai, samrā, mahāntam adhvānam eyan rathā vā nāvā vā samādatīta, evam evaitābhir upaniadbhih samāhitātmāsi, evam brndāraka āḍyah sann. adhīta-veda ukta upaniatkah, ito vimucyamānah kva gamiṣyasīti. nāham tad, bhagavan, veda, yatra gamiṣyāmīti; atha vai te 'ham tad vakyāmi, yatra gamiṣyasīti, bravītu, bhagavān,*

[8] For more of these examples see below.

iti.

As he descended from his divan, Janaka, the Videha king, spoke:
"I greet you, Yaknavalkya, please instruct me."
He (Yajnavalkya) replied:
"Your majesty, just as a man wishing to go on a long journey prepares a chariot or a boat, so you are united in spirit with the Upanishads, you are honored, wealthy, you have studied the Vedas and heard the Upanishads. Where will you go when released (from this body)?"
(Janaka) replied, "That, sir, I do not know, (i.e.) where will I go."
"Then, I will tell you this: Where you will go."
"Tell (me), sir."

4. *tasya prāco dik prāñcah prāṇāh, dadbhiṇā digdabhṇie prāṇāh, pratocī dik pratyañcah prāṇāh, udīcī digudañcah prāṇāh, urdhvā digurdhvāh prāṇāh, avācī digavāñcah prāṇāh, sarvā dišah sarve prāṇāh, sa ṣea neti netyātmā, argrhyo nahi grhyate, arṣīryo nahi šīryate, asaŋgo na hi sajhate, asito na vyathate na riṣyati; abhamayā vai janaka prāpto 'sīti hovāca yājñavalkyah. sa hovāca janako vaidehah, ubhayā tvā gacchatādyājñalkya yo no bhagavan nabhayā vedayse; namaste 'stuh; ime videhāh, uyamahamasmi. iti hitīyā brāhmaṇam.*

"Of him (i.e., the Rishi associated with the vital force = **prāṇāh**) the east is the eastern **prāṇāh**, the south the southern **prāṇāh**, the west the western **prāṇāh**, the north the northern **prāṇāh**, the upward **prāṇāh**, the downward **prāṇāh**, and all the directions (quarters), all the **prāṇāh**:

> they say (of) the **ātmā** 'it is not this', 'it is not that'; it is inconceivable, it is not grasped; indestructible it is not destroyed, unattached, it is not attached, it does not feel pain, it does not suffer injury."
> "You have gained that which is fearless, O Janaka!" said Yajnavalkya. And Janaka said, "Yajnavalkya, may that which is fearless be yours, for you have made that which is fearless known to us. Hail to you! This Videha [is yours], I myself am yours."

(Here the text even seems to equate **ātmā** with **prāṇāh**; the sharp distinction between the two seems to be a later development in this and other Upanishad texts.)

The division between body and *ātmā*' seems implicit in this text - "Where will you go when released (from this body)?" and " ...just like a man wishing to go on a long journey prepares a chariot or a boat..." which says in effect that the vital force does not cease to exist, does not lose its identity, but sets out on some further adventure. Nor is this a concept which originated with this particular thinker, it is rather one which reaches far back into the history of the human race itself. The belief that there is some essential part of man which exits the body at death and continues its existence as some essential spirit - some vital force - is already attested in the historical connections to other languages in the Indo-European family as we have seen in the etymological explanations above. The origins of the Sanskrit words - and their cognates in other languages - show its original connection to breath and breathing - and to the vital force or essence. In the history of Indian thought this connection came to be redefined in terms of the emerging concepts of time and being thus establishing the direction which speculation on the concept of this vital force would have to take for all the future. But thc primitive aspects of the concept of the vital force - those beliefs both inherited and borrowed - continue side by side with the new ideas. It is in this area that we find *vital force* conceived of as containing essentially those same character traits possessed by the living being from which it has departed, i.e., the philosophical speculations in which see the *vital force* in the context in which the nature of being and time are discussed remain the purview of the philosophers, while more popular speculation on the fate of the vital force adheres to the original view of a continuation of the individual in some spirit form. From this latter concept emerges - or continues - the concept of a realm of the dead where the departed vital forces may tarry, where misdeeds committed in life can be punished and good deeds rewarded as we have seen in the Vedic texts earlier. This, combined with the concept of metempsychosis (transmigration of the soul) promises that one's deeds in life will receive recognition after death and that, after the interval of punishment or reward, the vital force will find a new home appropriate to the actions in the previous life. The cycle of death and rebirth continues until the individuated vital force, cleansed of its bad deeds, is received into the ultimate well-spring and ultimate dwelling of all being.

> Die Stunde unseres Sterbens ist nur eine unserer Stunden und keine Ausnahmsweise.
>
> *Rainer Maria Rilke*

The Questions

In the Rig Veda we found the questions of *being*

and *time* stated more or less explicitly and answered perhaps equivocally, but certainly discussed in some detail and provided with suggestions for possible resolutions. The question on the ultimate fate of what we have preferred to call the 'vital force' is taken up in the Brahmanas and, in greater detail, in the Upanishads. What would seem to us today to be the first and, perhaps, most important question, i.e., does the vital force survive death, is not posed, but implicitly assumed to be a given: Yes, it does continue its existence. This, however, does summon up a number of additional questions which are extensively elaborated upon with citations from the teachings of the great Hindu thinkers. These questions are:

> What is the 'vital force'?
>
> How does it survive?
>
> If it is created then it may come to an end only to be created again or, if it is a part of a cycle of birth, death, and rebirth, an essentially atheistic concept, then it will come into being grow, perish, and be reborn. But, what becomes of the vital force in this process?
>
> As the vital force is equated to Brahma, what is Brahma and what is its relationship to the vital force?
>
> Does the vital force retain its individual identity, its knowledge, and its consciousness?

Defining the 'vital force': Tat tvam asi (you are this).

The vital force is that which is the 'life' in the living being. When the vital force departs life has departed. Here we find a distinction between 'life/living' and the vital force, which is the true, fundamental element of life, i.e., of the biological living being. The Chandogya Upanishad VI 11 explains this distinction using the living tree as the example of life. Life may depart from parts of the tree, but the tree lives on. When life (*ātma* or *prāṇāh*) has left the tree then the tree ceases to have life.

Chandogya Upanishad VI 11

1. *asya, saumya, mahato vrkasya yo mūle 'bhyāhanyādt, jīvan sravet; yo madhye 'bhydhanyāt, jīvan sravet yo 'gre 'bhyāhanyāt, jīvan sravet saṣeṣa jivenā 'tmanānuprabhūtah pepīyamāno modamānas tiṣṭhati.*

   Of this mighty tree, my lad, if someone should strike at the root it would bleed but still live: if someone should strike at the middle, it would bleed but still live. If someone should strike at the top, it would bleed but still live. Being pervaded by its living self, it exists, drinking in its moisture and rejoicing.

2. *asya yad ekā šākhā jīvo jahāti, atha sā šuṣyati, dvitīyā jahāti, atha sā šuyati, trtīyā̃ jahāti, atha sā šuṣyati, sarvā̃, jahāti sarvah šuṣyati, evam eva khalu, saumya, viddhi iti hovāca.*

   "If life leaves one branch of it, then it (that branch) dries up; if it leaves a second, then that dries up; if it leaves a third, then that dries up. If it leaves the whole, the whole dries up. Even so, indeed, my lad, understand," said he.

3. *jīvāpetam vāva kiledā̃ mriyate, na jīvo mriyata iti, sa ya eṣo' ṇimā aitad ātmyam idā̃ sarvā̃, tat satyam, sa ātmā, tat tvam asi, švetaketo, iti; bhūya eva mā, bhagzvān,*

vijñāpayatv iti; tathā, saumya, iti hovāca.

Truly, indeed, this body dies, when life has departed, but life itself does not die. That which is the subtle essence this whole world has for its *ātma*. That is the true. That is the *ātma*. That is you, Švetaketu. 'Please, Sir, instruct me further.' 'So be it, my lad,' he said.

The term *jīva* is used in the sense of the biological life of the individual as opposed to that element which gives life to the physical body, i.e., *ātmā* or *prāṇāh*. This survives the body and continues its existence. But this introduces the next, most significant question, i.e., what becomes of the departing 'vital force'.

How does the vital force survive?

This question takes on its own peculiar form in that it is explained such a way as to expand on the basic concept of the vital force. This vital force as an essence, as the element which gives the particular life to the individual, does not continue the awareness, the consciousness of the individual, but becomes absorbed into the greater vital force from which it arose and to which it ultimately owes its existence. This explanation introduces the very famous phrase '*tat tvam asi*' (that is you; i.e., what you are) which is to be found in virtually all religions arising out of these original speculations.

Chandogya Upanishad VI 9

1. *yathā, somya, madhu madhukrto nistiṣthanti, nānātyayānāim vrkṣāṇām rasā samavahāram ekatām*

rasam gamayanti.

Just, my lad, as bees prepare honey by collecting juices of different trees and reducing them into one essence.

2 *te yathā tatra na vivekam labhante, amuyāham vrkasya raso' smi, amuyāham vrkasya rasasmīti, evam eva khalu, saumya, imāh sarvāh prajāh sati sampadya na viduh, sati sampadyāmaha iti.*

And as these juices then do not make the distinction 'I am the juice of this tree, I am the juice of that tree,' indeed, my lad, all creatures, even though they have entered into being do not know that they have entered into being.

3. *taiha vyāghro vā sīho vā vrko vā varāho vā kīto vā patañgo vā dāšo vā mašako vā yad yad bhavanti, tad ābhavanti.*

They are here, tiger or lion or wolf or boar or worm or fly or gnat or mosquito, whatever they become, that they become.

4. *sa ya eo' imā aitadātmyam idam sarvā, tat satyā, sa ātmā, tat tvam asi, švetaketo, iti; bhūya eva mā, bhagzvān, vijñāpayatv iti; tathā, saumya, iti hovāca.*

That which is this fine essence, this all [world] belongs to itself. That is the true. That is the self. That is you, Shvetaketu. 'Please, Sir, instruct me still further.' 'So be it, my lad,' said he.

Chandogya Upanishad VI 10

1. *imah, saumya, nadyah purastāt prācyah syandante, paścāt pratīcyah tāh samudrāt samudram evāpiyanti, sa samudra eva bhavati, tā yathā tatra na viduh, iyam aham asmi, iyam aham asmīti.*

These rivers, my lad, flow, the eastern toward the east, the western, toward the west. They only go from sea to sea. They become the sea itself. Just as these rivers, while they do not know 'I am this one,' 'I am that one.'

2. *evam eva khalu, saumya, imāh sarvāh prajāh sata āgamya na viduh, sata āgacchāmaha iti, ta iha vyāghro vā sīho vā, vrko vā, varāho vā, kīto vi, patañgo vā, dā̃śo vā maśako vā, yadyad bhavanti tad ābhavanti.*

In the same manner, my lad, all these creatures even though they have come forth from being do not know that 'we have come forth from Being.' Whatever they are in this world, tiger or lion or wolf or boar or worm or fly or gnat or mosquito that they become.

3. *sa eo 'isimā aitad ātmyam idam sarvam, tat satyam, sa ātmā, tat tvam asi, śvetaketo, iti; bhūya eva mā, bhagavān vijñāpayatv iti; tathā, saumya, iti hovāca.*

That which is the subtle essence, this whole world has for its self. That is the true. That is the *ātmā.* That is you, Shvetaketu. 'Please, Sir, instruct me still further.' 'So be it, my lad,' said he.

Chandogya Upanishad 12

1. *Nyagradhaphalam ata āharet. idam, bhagavah iti.*

bhinddhīti. bhinnam, bhagavan, iti. kim atra paśsīti. avya ivemā dhānāh, bhagavah, iti. āsām aṅgaikā bhinddhīti. bhinnā, bhagavan, iti. kim atra paśyasīti. na kim cana, bhagavah, iti.

'Fetch me fruit from the *nyagrodha* tree.' 'It is done, Sir.' 'Split it.' 'It is split, Sir.' 'What do you see there?' 'These very fine grains, Sir.' 'Of these, please split one.' 'It is split, Sir.' 'What do you see there? 'Nothing at all, Sir.'

2. *tā hovāca yā vai, somya, etam aimānā na nibhālayase, etasya vai, somya, eo' imna evam mahān nyagrodhas tihati,*

Then he said to him, 'My lad, that finest part, [that] which you do not perceive, truly, my lad, from that part this great nygrodha tree exists.

3. *śrddhatsva, somya, sa ya eo' imnā, aitad ātmakam idā sarvā, tat satyam, sa ātmā, tat tvam asi, śvetaketo, iti. bhūya eva mā, bhagavān, vijñāpayatu iti. tathā, somya, iti. hovāca.*

That which is the finest part, all this [world], this essential part, this true part. This is the *ātmā* ness, That is you Švetaketu. 'Please, Sir, instruct me still further.' 'So be it, my lad,' he said.

Chandogya Upanishad 13

1. *lavaṇam etad udake' vadhāya, atha mā prār upasīdathā iti; sa ha tathā cakāra; tā hovāca: yad doṣā lavaṇam udake' vādhāh, aṅga tad āhareti, tadd hāvamrṣya na*

viveda; yathā vilīnam, evam.

Place this salt in water and bring it to me in the morning. He did so. Then (in the morning) he said to him, 'Please fetch that salt which you placed in water last evening.' But, having looked for it he did not find it for it was dissolved.

2. *aŋgāsyāntad ācāmeti: katham iti; lavaṇam iti; madhyād ācāmeti, katham iti; lavaṇam iti; āntad ācāmeti: katham iti; lavaṇam iti; abhiprāsyaitad atha mopāsīdathā iti; tadd ha tathā cakāra, tacchašvat sāvartate; tam hovāca: atra vāva kila sat, somya, na nibhālayase, atraiva kila.*

'Take a sip of it from this end.' He said, 'How is it?' 'Salty.' 'Take a sip from the middle. How is it?' 'Salty.' 'Take a sip from the other end. How is it?' 'Salty!' 'Put it aside and come to me.' He did so. 'It is homogeneous', and he said to him, 'Certainly, my lad, you do not comprehend, here is being, truly, it is here.'

3. *sa ya eṣo 'imā aitad ātmyam idā sarvām, tat satyam, sa ātmā, tat tvam asi, švetaketo, iti; bhūya eva mā, bhagavān, vijñāpayatv iti, tathā, somya, iti hovāca.*

What subtle essence this whole world has for its *ātmā*, that is the true. That is the *ātmā*. That is you, Švetaketu. 'Please, Sir, instruct me still further.' 'So be it, my lad,' he said.

How does the vital force survive? The answer is to be found in the preceding texts, but it seems ambiguous. The vital force is assimilated into all pervasive Brahma becoming a part of this - or continuing as a part of this, not knowing or remembering anything of its former character; as we see in the example of the rivers flowing into the sea where they no longer know their origin, or of the honey collected by the bees where honey from the individual sources no longer knows its source. But, from the Brhadaranyaka Upanishad, IV 2, 4:

Yajñavalkya replies:

> "Your majesty, just as a man wishing to go on a long journey prepares a chariot or a boat, so you are united in spirit with the Upanishads, you are honored, wealthy, you have studied the Vedas and heard the Upanishads. Where will you go when released (from this body)?"
> (Janaka) replied, "That, sir, I do not know, (i.e.) where will I go."
> "Then, I will tell you this: Where you will go."
> "Tell (me), sir."

And continues:

Of the Rishi associated with the vital force... the **ātmā** ' ...is not this', 'it is not that'; it is inconceivable, it is not grasped; (it is) indestructible it is not destroyed, unattached, it is not attached, it does not feel pain, it does not suffer injury.

All of which in some way seems to say that the **ātmā** retains its own unique identity though no longer attached to the body.

In the Upanishads the term *brahma(n)* has come to be the designation for the unnamed *tad ekam* of the Rig Veda X, 129, i.e., that which alone *was* at the beginning of time itself. The term occurred frequently in the Vedic texts where it is restricted in meaning to prayer, the power of prayer, the earnestness of prayer, and, finally, then to the lord of prayer, i.e., the one to whom prayer is directed, but in the Brahmanas and the Upanishads this last meaning is extended to the concept of the universal life force and the source of being and to being itself. Even here, however, this universal life force comes to be regarded also as a deva to be worshiped as are other devas, but given higher status as the supreme, the ultimate being. This development has a remarkable parallel in the Germanic word *god* which is directly related to the Vedic word *hū-*, *havate* (third person singular) 'call, summon.' The development moves from the meaning 'call, summon' to '*the one summoned*', but in the Germanic languages the thing summoned is more in line with that fundamental sense of the forces which control all life and are the forces of nature. In the Upanishads the new deity becomes the sole deity which, however, is not the only deity, and it also becomes the *all* itself from which everything which is originates and into which everything is ultimately absorbed, not only the source and the end of all that is, but existence itself.

In contemporary Hinduism the number of significant devas has been reduced to three (Shiva, Vishnu, and Brahma). Though Brahma is recognized as an important deva, one rarely finds temples or holy sites in India dedicated solely to this deva which would seem be the most important figure in Indian religion.

Taittriya Upanishad

1. ***prāṇo*** *brahmeti vyajānāt,* ***prāṇād*** *hy eva khalv imāni bhūtāni jāyante,* ***prāṇena*** *jītāni jīvanti,* ***prāṇam*** *pra-*

yanty abhisā višanti.
tad vījñāya, punar eva varuṇam pitaram upasasāra,
adhīhi bhagavo brahmeti.
tam hovāca, tapasābrahma vijijñāsasva, tapo brahmeti,
sa tapo tapyata, sa tapas taptvā

He observed, "Brahma is the **prāṇā** (the vital force)." Truly, these creatures (here) are born from **prāṇā** (the vital force) departing they enter into **prāṇā** (the vital force).
Having recognized this he again approached his father Varuna and said, "Sir, instruct me about Brahma."
He said to him, "Through asceticism try to know Brahma. Asceticism is Brahma."
He exercised asceticism; having exercised asceticism.

In resolving the dilemmas posed by the Hindu concepts of being and time Buddhist thinkers found a solution for the question of the fate of the vital force quite different from that of the authors of the Upanishads. In Buddhism everything that *is* emerges out of a convergence of *dharmas*, i.e., existence factors, eternal and indestructible, which work together, each originating in functional independence from the other, and then passing away to join into some new combination at a later time. This is not a simple concept: the dharmas are aspects of the universal dharma and are bearers each of its own unique characteristic, i.e., an irreducible 'particle' of a character trait. These combine to work together according to specific laws. In the characteristics of the individual five groups (*skandhas*) of dharmas compose the individual personality. The group (*rupa*) includes all elements, which form the material, physical

physical world of man and the world in which he lives. Four other skandhas are of invisible, spiritual character: vedana - the feelings of desire disinclination; *sangnya*: perception and imagination and the ability to distinguish between these; *sanskara* - the impulses for spiritual and moral activities; *vignyana* - consciousness. The interplay of these random traits make up the personality of the individual, but the dharmas are traits without any specific possessor, conditions, or subject which experiences them. Though they are unique, random traits the individual composed of these traits appears to possess some permanent indivisible personality even though in the spiritual realm these traits are in a continual state of change. Buddhism, therefore, rejects the notion of a permanent incorruptible 'soul', but nevertheless, accepts the belief in punishment through a series of rebirths for sins committed in the life of this specific personality (i.e., this particular combination of skandhas). Thus when the material and spiritual elements of the individual lose their connection and dissolve, the stream of conscious life stored by the *karma* does not cease, but persists after death forming the basis for the emergence of a new being which continues its life as heir to its deeds in the former life until it can achieve *nirvana*, i.e., release from the cycle of rebirths and reversion to the individual elements.

The End

The ideas on the nature of being and time of the ancient Hindu thinkers, though surely inaccessible to the ordinary human mind, early on became an integral part of Hindu thought and, as a consequence, concepts of the nature of the world and of the individual 'soul' were adjusted to take these difficult ideas into account. The basic tenants of the religions emerging from early Hinduism become the generally accepted explanations for the nature of the world, even though the previously held beliefs in an afterlife and of punishment in this afterlife for the sins of the individual persist, but are adjusted to accommodate the concept of the nature of being which is the basic principle of the religion.

In *About Time*[9] Paul Davies chides his contemporaries who do not seem to grasp the meaning of Stephen Hawking's theories on time and being, apparently overlooking in his criticism the impossibility of comprehending the incomprehensible and inconceivable. We, Davies contemporaries, are not at fault. These are concepts which no one can truly comprehend nor does it make any difference that we label this concept 'scientific' - as Davies does. The Hindu seers appear to be the first in the history of human thought to deal directly with this fundamental question in a manner similar to what we might approach it from today's perspective. They were able to accomplish this incredible intellectual feat in a culture, which surrounded them with a large array of deities, spirits, etc., and to focus on the problems which clearly conflict with traditional ideas. The assimilation of the thoughts introduced by the *kavis* of the Rig Veda, primarily in mandala 10 of the Rig Veda, also obliges later thinkers to resolve other questions which arise out of these original ideas, particularly that of the immortality of the human vital force. Given the difficulty in today's world of assimilating the most recent theories such as those of Einstein and Hawking one must wonder at the ability of the authors of the works of the Upanishads with their ability

[9]Davies, P. C. W. *About time: Einstein's unfinished revolution* / Paul Davies. New York: Simon & Schuster, 1995.

to grasp the significance of the speculations of the Rig Veda, to offer solutions to the problems these ideas presented, and to promulgate their own achievements. Though it is impossible to detail the spread of these ideas in the religions of the world, we find in these oldest sources the basic elements of most of the religions of the East - and, quite probably, of the fundamental elements in many of our western religions.

REFERENCE

Aufrecht, Theodor. Die Hymnen des Rig Veda (3rd ed.). 2 vols. Darmstadt: Wissenschaftliche Buchgesellschaft. 1955.

Balbir Singh. The Philosophy of Upanishads. Atlantic Highlands, NJ: Humanities Press. 1983.

Bolle, Kees W. (trsl.). The Bhagavadgītā; A New Translation. Berkeley: University of California Press. 1979.

Davies, P. C. W. About time: Einstein's unfinished revolution. New York: Simon & Schuster. 1995.

Dissanayake, Wimal. Introduction to Part Four. In: *Self as Person in Asian Theory and Practice*; Ed. Roger T. Ames with Wimal Dissanayake & Thomsa P. Kasulis. Albany, NY: State University of New York press. 1994.

Dumézil, Georges. Mitra-Varuna. New York: Zone Books. 1988.

Geldner, Karl Friedrich (Hrsg.). Der Rig-Veda. Cambridge MA: The Harvard University Press. Harvard oriental Series Vols. 33, 34, 35. 1951 ff.

Glasenapp, Helmuth von. Der Hinduismus; Religion und Gesellschaft im heutigen Indien. München: Kurt Wolf Verlag. 1922.

Glasenapp, Helmuth von. Von Buddha zu Gandhi. Tübingen: Verlag J. C. B. Mohr. 1934.

Glasenapp, Helmuth von. Die nichtchristlichen Religionen. Frankfurt a. M.: Fischer Bücherei. 1957.

Gonda, J. Change and Continuity in Indian Religion. The Hague: Mouton & Co. 1965.

Grassmann, Hermann. Wörterbuch zum Rig-Veda (3tte Auflage). Wiesbaden: Otto Harrassowitz. 1955.

Hardy, Edmund. Indische Religionsgeschichte. Leipzig: G. J. Göschen'sche Verlagshandlung. 1904

Hume, Robert E. The Thirteen Principal Upanishads. Translated from the Sanskrit. 2nd. Rev. edition. London: Oxford University Press. 1968.

Irwin, John (ed.). F. B. J. Kuiper, Ancient Indian Cosmogony. New Delhi: Vikas Publishing House pvt. Ltd. 1983.

James, E. O. Creation and Cosmology. Leiden: E. J. Brill. 1969.

James, E. O. Myth and Ritual in the Ancient Near East. Lonodn: Thames and Hudson. 1958

James, E. O. The Worship of the Sky God. London: Anthlone Press, University of London. 1963.

Long, Charlotte R. The Twelve Gods of Greece and Rome. Leiden: E. J. Brill.1987

Lorenz, Kuno. Indische Danker. München: C. H. Beck'sche Verlags-buchhandlung. 1998

Maurer, Walter H. (ed. and trsl.). Pinnacles of India's Past; Selections from the Rigveda. Amsterdam: John Benjamins Publishing Company. 1986.

Miller, Jeanine. The Vision of Cosmic Order in the Vedas. London: Routledge & Keagan Paul. 1985.

Monier-Williams, Monier. Brāhmanism and Hindūism; or, Religious Thought and Life in India, as based on the Veda and other sacred books of the Hindus. 4th ed. New York : Macmillan and Co. 1891.

Oldenberg, Hermann. Religion des Veda. Stuttgart und Berlin: J. G. Cotta'sche Buchhandlung Nachfolger. 1923.

O'Flaherty, Wendy Doniger. The Rig Veda; An Anthology. Harmonsworth: Penguin Books. 1981.

Radhakrishnan, S. The Principal Upaniads; edited with introduction,. text, translation, and notes by S. Radhakrishnan. London: George Allen & Unwin Ltd. 1953.

Raj, Sundar M. Time. Rg Vedic Studies. Series III. Madras: International Society for the Investigation of Ancient Civilization. 1983.

Roth, R. & Whitney, W. D. (hrsg.). Arthava Veda Sanhita (3tte Auflage). Bonn: Hannover: Ferd. Dümmlers Verlag. Reprint 1956.

Schmitt, Rüdiger. Dichtung und Dichtersprache in indogermanischer Urzeit. Wiesbaden: Otto Harrassowitz. 1967.

Sharma, Arwin. The Hindu Gītā. London: Gerald Duckworth & C. Ltd. 1986.

Sinha, Phulgenda. The Gita As It Was. La Salle, Illinois: Open Court. 1987.

Swāmī Mādhavānanda (trsl.). The Brhadārayaka Upaniad. Calcutta: Advaita Ashrama. 1965.

Swāmī Nikhilananda. Man in Search of Immortality. London:
George Allen and Unwin. 1968.

Van den Broek, R.; Baarda, T.; and Mansfield, J. Knowledge of God in

the Graeco-Roman World. Leiden: E. J. Brill. 1988.
Vedavyas, Dr. Science of Time. Hyderabad: University of Sciences. 1997.
Welbon, Guy Richard. The Buddhist Nirvāna and its Western Interpreters. Chicago: The University of Chicago Press. 1968.